UNLOCKING THE JOSHUA ANOINTING

Ayeisha Kirkland

ISBN 9798218269036

Unless otherwise noted, all scriptures are from the King James Version, public domain.

I have three dedications for this book.

To the **Kingdom of God**,
I dedicate this book to your advancement.
This is for the honor of Almighty God and the spreading of
the Gospel of Jesus Christ.

To my grandmother, **Clarita Cruickshank**.
You introduced me to the faith.
That was the start of my Kingdom purpose.

To **YouthForChrist305+**.
You allowed me to be your leader.
My experiences with you all taught me the lessons that I share in this
book.

Allow me to express my deepest gratitudes for every person that played a role in the publication of this book:

Inspired by:

The Holy Spirit

Edited by:

Samantha Hardy-Shortridge Ed.S

Copy Edited by:

Jerod Bellamy, Makalah Tyler, Emmanuel Joseph, Missy L'Esperance, Natalie Mathurin, and Khouri Robinson

Cover Designed by:

All Things Cre8

Back Cover Photo by:

Musiqool Media

Special Thanks To

1. My Mother, **Ingrid Cruickshank** for her selfless dedication to my godly upbringing and her constant support of my Kingdom calling.

2. **New Alpha Worship Center** for its constant support, love, and prayer.

3. **Apostle Errol and Pastor Angela Williams**, who pulled out what God put in me.

4. **Christian Williams,** my mentor who constantly pours into me, and **Niketa Williams-Cherilus,** whose obedience to the prophetic call on her life made this book possible.

5. **Ken Isidore**, for always being there for me.

CONTENTS

FOREWORD

I will never forget the Sunday morning. Right before the service started, my office door was knocked on. I answered the door to a kind grandmother with her "wide-eyed" granddaughter. The child stood there with a penetrating glance. I thought that they just wanted to say hello to their pastor. I realized that was not the case.

When "grandma" introduced her 8-year-old granddaughter to me, she said, "pastor, my granddaughter wants to be baptized". I was taken aback. I was super surprised. After getting past being shocked that an 8-year-old would ask for water baptism, I went on to have a brief interview with who I know now as the young evangelist. I am talking about Ayeisha Kirkland, the author of this book.

Even though I did not see exactly how at the time, as her pastor, I had a gut feeling that Ayeisha was unique in many ways. I noticed that she was more focused, serious, and obedient than her peers as she continued to attend church. She rarely missed Sunday school or Bible study, and even on school days, she frequently completed her homework assignments while she listened in another room.

Parents are told by God in His word to "Train up a child in the way he should go: and when he is old, he will not depart from it" (Proverbs 22:6). The book you are holding in your hands is the outcome of this command. It is also a by-product of prophecy from God. In *Unlocking*

The Joshua Anointing, the author clearly presents the heartbeat of God for the younger generation.

I am humbled and greatly honored to be asked to write the foreword to this magnificent, life-changing, and thought-provoking book. It will unlock many sought after truths.

Apostle Errol Williams,
Senior Pastor, New Alpha Worship Center
Author, *Struck By The Silent Killer*

INTRODUCTION

On July 29, 2012, a bright, breezy Sunday morning, I was baptized. This was not my initiation into a denomination. My goal was not to show others that I became a member of a fancy religion; instead, I publicly showed a number of witnesses that I received and properly responded to a revelation (an unveiled truth) from God. At eight years old, I became aware that there was, is, and is to come, a God who created the world and its inhabitants. I learned that He desired a relationship with the people He created. I realized this creator was thinking about me before I physically had the ability to think. He knew what was best for me then and still does now. All He wanted to do was lead me. He already chose me; however, we could not be in a relationship until I chose him.

That is what I did! I chose Him through confessing with my mouth and believing in my heart that He was Lord. After, I got baptized because that was His standard of unapologetically declaring my new relationship with Him to those around me. I was not old or wise enough at that time to comprehend the full extent of my decision, nor did I have the foresight to see where this decision would take me. I did not enter into a relationship with God with strings attached. I did not have any demands or expectations. All I had was an intentional desire to follow His way, since I was convinced it was the best way for me to take.

The more I followed His way, the more I realized it entailed more than what I was aware of. I understood I had to go to church, and put something in the offering basket. I knew I had to tell others about Jesus, but I never knew I had a calling. I did not know that there was a particular job assigned to me that God expected me to complete on Earth. Never did I see myself as one who had a specific purpose that would affect the lives of others. Once I began to realize it, I always thought I was too young to fulfill it at my current age. I was convinced I had to wait until I matured physically before I could walk in the purpose that God prescribed to me.

Eleven years after my baptism, I now stand as the founder of Youth-ForChrist305+, a Miami-based, global network of christian teenagers that has reached over three hundred youth and young adults through evangelism, revitalization, education, and cultivation. God has blessed us to be a blessing to our community near and far. As this ministry's leader, I've been recognized for its community impact by the Miami Herald (one of the most revered newspapers in Miami), the City of Miami Mayor, and the City of Miami Police Department among others. Nothing has been more rewarding than to see the individual lives impacted, as we pull youth out of the world and support them in the process of becoming pillars of the faith to those around them.

How did I get here? I did not get here by divine planning, but I was led here through intentional obedience. One of the things I wish I had before I arrived here was a greater understanding of what I was walking into. When no one has done what you are doing at the magnitude and age level you are doing it at, it is extremely difficult to find someone to identify with. For this reason, I was ill prepared for the obstacles I faced. I found myself wanting to quit many times because I did not have the proper content as to what I was experiencing. This is why I wrote this book. Every page is what I wish I heard on my journey. This book is not a cheat code to the process, nor is it a supplement to the supreme word of God through The Holy Bible. This book is a complement for young Christian leaders (especially those in ministry) to read, so they can deepen their understanding. The more one understands the assignment, the closer they get to the purpose God has for them!

I feel like Paul in Ephesians 1:18-19. As you read this book, I pray "the eyes of your understanding being enlightened; that ye may know the hope of His calling" on your life. I will not only share what the word of God says about this particular calling but also my transparent, tragic mistakes and tremendous, triumphant successes to give you both a biblical and real-world context into the assignment on your life. As you read, you will be given keys to unlock the Joshua anointing. Don't be like the Pharisees in Jesus' day who received the keys and did not open up the doors (Luke 11:52). As you put into action what you have learned, I believe you will unlock a greater level of anointing by the end of this book!

Let's grow!
Ayeisha Kirkland

1

WHEN DO I START?

There are many books of the Bible named after the respective characters they describe. From world-class women of God like Ruth and Esther to powerful prophets like Hosea, Ezekiel, and Daniel, there are several Bible characters you can learn about by solely reading about the books named after them. However, Joshua is an outlier. Even though you can learn about Joshua through the book named after him, it is imperative to note that only reading the book of Joshua gives you a limited perspective about who he was. It is like trying to reach to the top level of a building but neglecting the stairs or an elevator. That is foolish! It is faulty to be consumed with a desired destination, but dismissive of the directions needed to get to that place. Sadly, this is exactly what many believers in the body of Christ look like. They are hungry to reach a new level but unwilling to go through the unavoidable process to reach that place.

In Joshua 1:2, God commanded Joshua to:

"Now Therefore Arise!"

Because we are living in a time where Twitter is a primary way of communicating, and the microwave is the go-to device to reheat food, we are accustomed to things being short and quick. Brevity is our expectation. When we put an address in our GPS, most times we look for the fastest possible route. We are even willing to pay tolls to get somewhere quicker than other routes require, as long as we get there the fastest. Similarly, for many believers, brevity is desired in the spiritual realm. Being hasty for aspired spiritual destinations is costing us. I know you want to "arise"; however, it is dangerous to shorten that clause into one word. If we only read "arise", we fixate on the command to walk in the calling, but neglect words like "now" and "therefore". These foolishly disregarded words indicate that there is a set time that follows the completion of prerequisites for a believer to walk in their assignment. Something needs to occur first:

An Unlocking Needs To Happen!

Unlocking is the act of using a key to authenticate or prove one has access to the full functionality of something. Unlocking does not provide brand new material. It just provides entrance to materials already provided. No matter who you are, saved or unsaved, you need to know that there is an anointing, which is a distinct calling from God that is empowered by His Spirit, upon your life. This calling and the empowerment given by the Spirit to walk in that calling was provided for you before you were born. It is already in you! You just have to uncover it, so you can walk in it.

The Bible informs us that, "We are his workmanship, created in Christ Jesus for good works, which God prepared ahead of time for us to do" (Ephesians 2:10 CSB). This means you are not a mistake or an accident, but you are God's personal, handcrafted, work of art. He desired and positioned you before you were born to be on display for His purpose and "His pleasure" (Revelation 4:11). When speaking to Jeremiah, God told him "I chose you before I formed you in the womb; I set you apart before you were born. I appointed you a prophet to the nations" (Jeremiah 1:5 CSB). God is not a respecter of persons (Romans 2:11): more specifically, He does not care for any of us more than the other. In the same way He chose Jeremiah, He chose you before you were formed, and set you apart and appointed you for a particular calling. I do not know what your calling may be, but I know whatever He has called you to do, He already put it on the inside of you. You just need to go through a growth process, like a seed grows into a tree, in order to unlock and access the anointing He gave you.

This book is specifically for those who believe they have a Joshua anointing. Although I will provide more context as to what that is over the course of this book, the simple definition of the Joshua anointing that we will be exploring is the **calling and empowerment from God to lead others in your generation**. This book is meant to touch young leaders, and leaders of youth who have leadership potential. This book is not a bible study on the book of Joshua, but a guide that explains principles on which Joshua based his ministry. As you read this book, you will be provided with different aspects of Joshua's life to properly understand the nature of his calling and the necessary steps one must take to unlock that anointing. This is why we are not starting at Joshua chapter one! We do not only want to know when he got to the top floor, but we want to see the steps he took to get there. The question arises: what was Joshua's true beginning?

2

WHOM DO I FEAR?

It is my belief that the first thing Joshua developed in order to unlock his anointing was fear. Some would consider fear to be a strange key, but it is only because they are oblivious to the type of fear I am referring to. In this context, fear is not the act of being cowardly, but the origin of conviction. It is the by-product of knowing God, and consequently the gas that fuels a desire to learn more about Him.

Fear is the act of "regarding with reverence and awe". In simple words, someone you fear is someone who you deeply respect. You hold them to a particular standard, and because of that, your behavior responds to your belief in them. To make it clear, I want you to think about a physical church building. There are certain acts that people do not commit in a physical church building due to the respect they have for the church. For example, using profanity and committing sexual immorality are abominable acts within themselves. Based on societal morality standards, these offenses would be considered more gross if they were done in a church building. This is a result of the respect that people have for the church. The same respect is held for pastors, parents, and particular leaders. There are certain things that you do not do in the presence of these individuals out of respect for them.

Reverence is already in the DNA of every human being, but this reverence needs to be directed to the right spiritual entity.

Whom Do You Fear?

Everything that you do is out of fear for someone. No human being is led by themselves. Rather, every human being is a sponge, sucking up the thoughts, desires, and emotions of another spirit. There are three things you need to know about spirits:

1. You are a spirit, with a soul, that contains a mind, a will, and emotions. You are housed in a body.
(1 Thessalonians 5:23)
2. God is a Spirit, who also has a soul, that is joined with your spirit once you become a believer in Jesus.
(John 4:24, 1 Corinthians 6:17, Romans 8:16)
3. There is an enemy working against humanity and the will of God named the Devil. He has a number of spirits called demonic spirits that dominate the unbeliever and constantly targets the believer in an attempt to undermine them.
(John 10:10, 1 John 4:1-4, Ephesians 6:12)

Now that you have this information, you must understand that your spirit never acts alone. It is either led by the spirit of God as a son of God or dominated and driven by a demonic spirit (Romans 8:14, John 8:44). Every action has a "spiritual motive": an origin spirit that encourages the behavior. You should never judge a person for the actions they commit because people are mere vessels. They are empty containers for another spirit to fill. In reference to this, the prophet Jeremiah shared that "I know, Lord, that a person's way of life is not his own; No one who walks determines his own steps" (Jeremiah 10:23 CSB). This means that if a person who does not know Jesus is committing abominable actions, they are being dominated and driven by a spirit that persuades that behavior. They, like us, need an encounter with Jesus to be free. Once we get in a relationship with Jesus, we now have a choice as to what spirit we are led by. Before meeting Jesus, we are dominated by demonic spirits from birth. After meeting Jesus, we are dominated by demonic spirits by choice.

Every spirit has a soul with a mind, will, and emotions. Spirits think, desire, and feel. Then, spirits communicate what they are thinking, desiring, and feeling to the human being they are leading or dominating. Both the Holy Spirit and demonic spirits communicate with you. Our thoughts do not even originate from us. You get to decide what thoughts you want to keep or get rid of. Paul elaborates on this in 2 Corinthians 10:5 by informing us that believers have the ability to "Cast down imaginations, and bring into captivity every thought into the knowledge of Christ" (2 Corinthians 10:5). The thoughts we have are seeds planted by spirits, and we dictate if we let those seeds grow or not. When the enemy comes sowing weeds, do you water them, or do you uproot them? When God sows seeds into you, are you killing them through lack of care for them or catering to them so they can bear fruit?

The way you respond to a voice determines if you fear or respect the person that the voice came from. If you obey what a person commands you to do, you fear them. Failure to comply with someone's orders is an indication that you do not respect them. For example, if your parents tell you to do something and you ignore their command, you do not respect them. Substitute teachers get this kind of treatment. A regular teacher and a substitute could ask the same thing of a student, but the regular teacher is more likely to get compliance because of the respect students have for their regular teacher compared to a substitute. In the historical Chinese Confucian system, they have a system called filial piety. It was a system where subordinates had to deeply respect and obey the ones set over them. An example includes a son needing to respect and obey their father.

In order for you to walk in any calling that God has on your life, you have to fear Him. You must respect Him in order to listen when He speaks to you. If you do not obey God, it is because you fear someone else. You have more respect for the demonic spirit that instructed you to disobey. Misguided reverence will threaten your ability to evolve as a leader.

How Do I Hear The Voice f God?

A failure to obey God is tantamount to rejecting the purpose He has for you. God is not forceful, but God is a gentleman. The book of Revelation records Him as one who stands at the door and knocks (Revelation 3:20). If you were expecting God to kick down the door of your life and force you to embrace your assignment, you are greatly mistaken. Someone who knocks is expecting permission to come in and do what He desires. You have free will; more specifically, you have the legal right according to the way God designed you to choose His purpose or that of your own. You can attempt to walk with God without walking in the calling He gave you. However, that walk will be difficult. Being outside of the purpose He has for you is loathsome. You cannot be truly satisfied when you're not walking in the purpose He created you for. Something will always feel like it is missing.

My Personal Experience

In my case, becoming a youth leader was NOT my preference. It was not something I gave an automatic yes to. Back then, if I knew I would end up where I am now, I most likely would have run away a long time ago. Before I embraced the calling, I was living the life I preferred. I was in pursuit of a career in rap and poetry. I was writing, recording, creating content for social media, and performing all over my city. I got to perform on the biggest performing-arts stage in my state in front of 2,000 people. I received notable invitations from influential people in my county to share my voice at revered functions. My music and poetry were not demonic. A majority of my catalog was gospel. The pieces that had other subjects like suicide awareness, voting, and black history still highlighted Jesus. One can say I was doing a godly thing. I had to learn that just because something is godly, that does not mean it is God-ordained for me at that time!

After making a song with former NFL player Chad Thomas who now became a well-recognized rapper in Miami by the name of Major Nine, I gained a lot of attention in the music industry. I recall my friends being desperate to know my next move. They were curious as to how I was going to capitalize off that publicity. As I started to reflect, I heard God speak clearly. He told me to "stop pursuing the music because it is NOT my final destination for you. Start pursuing Me and you will see what I have in store for you." This was not what I wanted to hear! I had an expectation to do what I wanted! When I finally got to a point that looked promising for me to attain all the attention the music scene had to offer me, God requested of me to deny that life and embrace where He was sending me. It did not matter if I carried His name while I did music, because that is not where He wanted me to be. In the same way, carrying Jesus' name but not carrying out His commands makes you a counterfeit! Just because you own a Lebron Jersey does not make you a Laker player. It is more than wearing the name. It is all about being identified in the right place with the right posture. This will ensure your spiritual prosperity as you go through the process. This was not a simple decision, but it was one I had to make. I could not fear my music goals more than the God who gave me my musical talent.

I am confident that Joshua had his own will. Even Jesus had his own will. Jesus shares that "I came down from Heaven, not to do mine own will, but the will of him that sent me" (John 6:38). This tells me that Jesus, because He was a human, had human desires. The Bible shares He came in sinful flesh (Romans 8:28). It is human nature to want to do your own thing. We would rather our preference over something else that requires us to sacrifice what we want. Jesus even requested to deny the cross (Matthew 26). Not only is the assignment that God has for you something that you may not prefer, but it will be painful and gruesome at times. This is true for leadership especially. We think it is beneficial to be in charge. Everybody wants to be the boss because they are ignorant of what is required. Behind closed doors, the pursuit of exhibiting effective, impactful, godly leadership characteristics is detrimental to one's personal desires. You can only choose this life out of fear. If you don't revere God, you will not choose the calling He has for you. Despite Jesus not wanting to get on the cross, He rebutted "Nevertheless, not my will, but thy will be done" (Matthew 26). Only fear, a deep respect for the one over you, enables you to say "nevertheless."

How Do I Attain Fear?

Jesus shared, "Every branch in me that beareth fruit, He purgeth it, that it might bring forth more fruit" (John 15:2). In the kingdom of God, we start with a small amount of something. Overtime, the small amount we have will eventually increase if we properly respond to the process. At this point, you only need mustard seed fear to start. The bigger fear will come eventually. You need to respect God more than social media when He leads you to read the Bible instead of scrolling endlessly for hours. You need to respect God more than a person when He leads you to hang up the phone and go into prayer. As you take small steps, you will develop more fear in the process.

3

WHY ME?

One of the things people ignorantly disregard about a relationship with God is the fact that it is general and personal. Relationships are both general and personal. First, we will break down the fact that relationships are general. Many people have spouses. There are general, or universal rules everyone should adhere to in a biblically designed marriage. These include unity, fidelity, sacrifice, respect, commitment, and of course love. I want it to be understood that biblical marriages all over the world have similarities; however, just because they have things in common does not mean they do everything the same. Next, we will break down the fact that relationships are personal. Not every husband and wife live in the same type of homes, drive the same type of cars, or divide household responsibilities in the same manner. It is faulty to require every husband-and-wife relationship to be exactly the same because unique types of people develop unique types of relationship preferences. Imagine if every husband and wife had to wear the same type of clothes, work the same kind of jobs, and go to the same type of restaurants. We would be missing a factor that God sought fit to embed into mankind: diversity. Many in the body of Christ discourage diversity because they falsely think it is a threat to unity.

United Does Not Mean Identical

Just like the example with marriages, a relationship with God is also general and personal. There are common foundational aspects you must find in every relationship with God such as reading the Bible, praying, fasting, giving, and more. Individually, you begin to see God requiring certain things from people, but those demands are not given to the entire Body of Christ. God doesn't require everyone to pray for the same amount of time, and God does not require everyone to read the same amount of Scriptures daily. Just because Moses fasted for forty days and forty nights twice does not mean Jesus had to do so twice. Jesus only did it once while Esther fasted for three days only. This is just one small example of how God has a general standard for all His people, but He deals with the execution of that general standard on an individual basis.

Another way God displays the General-Personal Principle is in His various ways of determining righteousness. Righteousness is the quality of man being in right standing with God. Scripture testifies of four different ways people obtained righteousness from God throughout the Bible. The way they obtained righteousness depended on the era they were living in. To illustrate this, we are going to discuss what I like to call the "Four Eras of Righteousness".

1. Formed-Righteous Era

This first era was short-lived. It means that mankind during this time did not have to do anything to receive righteousness because they came into the world righteous. You can read about it in Genesis 2-3. Only Adam and Eve got to experience this kind of righteousness. It was the heart of God for every man to be born righteous, in the same way Adam and Eve were formed that way. They did not have to worry about obtaining it, but simply maintaining it. There was only one command they had to follow to ensure they stayed in right standing with God: do not eat off of the tree of knowledge of good and evil. When they ate that fruit, they acted in disobedience. This sin caused them to lose their righteousness. They were kicked out of the Garden as a result. Sin is notorious for being a threat to righteousness. To learn more about this, refer to Romans 6:23 and Isaiah 59:2. Not only did Adam and Eve lose Eden; consequently, the entire human race lost the right to come into the world in right standing with God (Romans 5:12).

2. Counted-Righteous Era

Romans 5 confirms that after Adam, every man was born into sin, even if they did not commit a sin themselves, because they generationally inherited the sin nature from Adam and Eve (Romans 5:12-14). However, men like Enoch, Noah, and Abraham stood out to God during this era for being righteous. If they were born into sin and unrighteousness, what did they do to obtain righteousness?

Genesis 5 describes Enoch as one who "walked with God" (Genesis 5:24). He was translated instead of mortalized. This means he did not die a physical death but was received by God into heaven automatically while he was still living. Fun fact: the only other man to do that was Elijah in 2 Kings 2.

Genesis 6 describes Noah as a man who "Found grace in the eyes of the Lord" (Genesis 6:8). He was also "A just man and perfect in his generations" (Genesis 6:9). Similar to Enoch, the Bible shares that "Noah walked with God" (Genesis 6:9). He feared God enough to build a boat at a time when it never rained. That boat saved his entire family from a flood.

Lastly, Genesis 12 – 22 highlights the experiences of Abraham. He was a man who feared God. He forsook everything he knew to follow God to a place unrevealed. He had faith that God would give him a son at over 70 years old. Once he finally received that son named Isaac, he feared God enough to nearly sacrifice Isaac when God requested. This is because he chose to honor God over his preference. God did not really want Abraham to kill his son, He just wanted to see if he was willing to do it. God stopped him in the middle of the process.

These are just three examples of several men in the book of Genesis after Adam and before Moses who did not have a prescribed law to follow but were still called righteous by God. I am personally convinced that this is because of their faith. Paul quotes Genesis 15:6 in Romans 4 to share how Abraham received righteousness. Paul reiterates that "Therefore his faith was credited to him [Abraham] as righteousness (right standing with God)" (Romans 15:6 AMP). I believe faith was the standard that made these great men of God righteous during this time. Recall that both Enoch and Noah walked with God. Other Bible characters such as Abraham, Isaac, Jacob, and Joseph also walked with God through their choice to forsake their way to follow God's way. According to Paul, walking with God requires one to "walk by faith and not by sight" (2 Corinthians 5:7). Enoch could not live righteously, while the world grew desperately wicked, without faith.

Noah could not build a boat, during a time it never rained, without faith. Isaac, Jacob, and Joseph could not obey God, in the ambitious ways they did, without faith. Walking with God requires you to have a belief in what God is saying. Since all these men were men of faith, I believe that they too received the righteousness Abraham received. Their faith was counted to them as righteousness.

3. Law-Righteous Era

The next two eras that will be discussed are the ones that are most familiar. Many believe they are the only two eras that exist. The first of these was instituted by Moses. The foundation of it includes the famous Ten Commandments. This is when God gave mankind a set of rules that they must abide by to obtain their righteousness. If they broke those rules, righteousness was lost. To regain righteousness, God created a system of animal sacrifice. The people were to take a lamb without spot or blemish and bring it to the priest. The priest would then act as a proxy on behalf of the people and offer the sacrifice before God. If God accepted the sacrifice, they would regain their righteousness. To read more about this, reference Leviticus 9. This era continued until the death of Jesus Christ, the final, eternal sacrifice for man's sin.

4. His Righteousness Era

This is the current era that we are living under. It will not be replaced. It follows closely after the Law-Righteous Era. It requires a spotless lamb. It requires a sacrifice to be made by a priest for the atonement of sin. However, lambs are not the sacrifice and man is not the priest. Christ became both the priest and the lamb. He offered Himself as a sacrifice for the atonement of our sins. To read more about this, reference Hebrews 8-9. Paul describes this ministry by sharing, "For he hath made him to be sin for us, who knew no sin; that we might be made the righteousness of God in him" (2 Corinthians 5:20). No longer do we work for our righteousness through obedience to a law, but we are made righteous through His sacrifice alone and our belief in His sacrifice (Ephesians 2:8-9).

Personal Execution Of General Principles

As you can see from these four different examples, there were distinct ways God gave righteousness to mankind depending on the time they lived in. I want to make it very clear that even though God has a different way of doing things over time, it does not mean God changes Himself. In reference to Himself, God shares, "For I am the Lord, I change not" (Malachi 3:6). He is referenced as being the "Same yesterday, today, and forever" (Hebrews 13:8). God does not reinvent Himself to different people. There are common themes, but different ways those same themes are expressed. Each of the four eras had similarities. God still required faith, obedience, and righteousness in each era. He is not doing away with His principles but establishing them to different people in a personal way.

God Will Be Personal With You!

You may have one of two types of responses to what you just read. If you are a bible nerd like me, you may be enthralled with this type of teaching. However, another group may be thinking, "What does this have to do with being a young leader?". Young Joshuas must understand that God is a personal God, because God requires personal things from them that He is not asking of anyone else. Jesus emphasized to His followers that, "To whom much is given, much is required" (Luke 12:48). There will be times when you might step back and say "God this is too much for me! Why do I have to carry this and no one else does?".

Joshua On The Mountain

Joshua was doing things that no other person in Israel had to do. Joshua was Moses' minister. See, the modern church makes us think a minister is someone with a title who functions in some type of leadership. This is contrary to what scripture explains. Scripture describes a minister as a servant. It is a person who is similar to a waiter in a restaurant. Their responsibility is to cater to the desire of who they serve. Joshua had to wait on Moses and cater to his personal desires. Anything Moses needed; Joshua was required to attend to those needs. One example is found in Exodus 24, "And Moses rose up, and his minister Joshua: and Moses went up into the mount of God. And he said unto the elders, Tarry ye here for us, until we come again unto you: and, behold, Aaron and Hur are with you: if any man have any matters to do, let him come unto them" (Exodus 24:13-14). God wanted Moses to commune with Him for 40 days and 40 nights alone. All the children of Israel could not come, but Joshua was allowed to go with Moses. He was actually required to go because of his assignment as a minister. Let's make this realistic. Joshua was a young man at the time. While Moses and Joshua were on that mountain, the children of Israel built the golden calf. They threw a party (Exodus 32). Joshua couldn't turn up with his friends. He could not do what everybody else was doing, but he had to be set apart! Being set apart was a requirement for his assignment.

Joshua served in other capacities before he became Moses' replacement. Alongside being Moses' minister, Joshua was spy of the land of Israel (Numbers 14:8,16). He also served as the leader of the army that fought against the Amalekites (Exodus 17:9-13). I wonder if Joshua ever felt overwhelmed. It would seem as if Moses wanted him to do everything. The reality is, God put Joshua on the mind of Moses for different positions so he can practice for his future assignment. His distinct journey is what made him worthy of being Moses' replacement.

My Personal Experience

In the same way Joshua missed the party to be on the mountain, I have been required to do many things that even my Christian friends are not required to do. People fail to realize Joshua did not stand out in a crowd of sinners, but he was distinct among the children of Israel. It is one thing to do things differently than your worldly friends, but there is a different type of hurt that arises when God requires you to be different from your Christian friends. There have been seasons where God publicly used prophets to tell me "Now is not the time for a boyfriend," while my other Christian friends were allowed to date. There would be moments when my Christian friends went out and most of the time I could not make it because God told me to attend church services. God would assign me to minister during birthday parties. Joshuas tend to miss parties. Sometimes I would promise to go out with them, but God will tell me the day of, "Just stay home and pray." I found myself in seasons where I could not do what others were doing nor could I consume what others were digesting because God had an assigned diet for me. The anointing has a diet attached to it! Like Samson, Samuel, and John the Baptist as Nazirites, the young

Joshua will be assigned to consecrate in ways that are only for them (Judges 13, 1 Samuel 1:11, Matthew 3:4).

I also identify with Joshua in reference to having a lot of assignments. In my local church, New Alpha Worship Center, I currently serve in many functions. I serve as a Sunday school teacher, youth leader, and a radio host. Ever since I joined the church, I have found myself doing a lot of things that people do not even know I do. There have been times where I assist in cleaning the sanctuary. I have done plenty of graphic designing work. I have taught Bible studies, preached Sunday sermons, been looked upon to pray for the sick, and released several prophetic words. This is just a taste of all the Kingdom work I have done. I am sharing it with you to demonstrate that I identify with feeling like I have been asked to do too much.

Get An Understanding

Maybe you are already at a crossroad because you have already been asked by God to do things that you feel like He was only asking you. If you are anything like me, you might be using the fact that others are not doing it as an excuse to disobey. Why am I not allowed to date when others can? If they can do it, I can do it as well. That is not how God works. Our standard for obedience is not other believers, it is God himself. Joshua couldn't say, "If my friends do not have to go on the mountain, I do not have to either."

Do not feel like you are being left out. I definitely felt like that for a long time. It is not isolation, but separation. You are not lonely, but in solitude. Those definitions are distinct. One is meant to implicate lack while another is meant to indicate contentment. Learn to be content with what God is personally requiring of you, because it is making you into who God has called you to be. Understanding this will enable you to be okay with the season you are in. You will realize that you won't be who God has called you to be unless you submit to the personal requirements.

This is not permission to be prideful and have a false consolation. Many in this situation comfort themselves with self-absorbed conclusions that "They are more anointed." No one is more anointed than anyone. Some just tap into it more than others. Do not use this moment to say things like "Many are called but few are chosen." True understanding of Matthew 22 will make you realize that everyone is called with a chance to be chosen. Few are chosen because only few accept, not because few are *better*. One thing that I truly repent of is condemning my friends for doing things because God told me not to do them. When God urged me to not date anyone, I was quick to point the finger at others' relationships and find fault. Do not let bitterness turn you into a judge. Now, because people are doing things that God said you can't, you consider them heathens and yourself an angel. The reality is, you cannot concern yourself with others. According to Matthew 7, this road that you are on is called the "strait and narrow" (Matthew 7:13-14). This means that the road is a tiny space, with little to no clearance for someone to be next to you. It does not mean you are lonely, but it means there is no room to look left and right. When God is speaking to you, remove what others are doing from the conversation. Instead of saying "Why me?", change that to "Why not me?". Take it up a notch and tell God, "Thank God it is me!". God reassures us in Romans 8 that "All things work together for those who love the Lord, and those called according to His purpose." (Romans 8:28). In other words, everything you are going through right now is instrumental to your destiny. Obey Him and watch where He takes you.

4

WHERE ARE YOU?

Before we transition into the second key that unlocks a young leader, I want to quickly summarize what was discussed so far. In essence, we learned that upcoming young leaders have a choice to make; we can either choose to obey God's voice in reverence or ignore His voice in disrespect. We acknowledged that sometimes we do not want to honor His voice because we feel like we are being singled out. However, we concluded that obeying God's voice is critical to our destiny. In this next chapter, we will closely examine another reason why obeying God's voice is important.

The voice of God is primarily a source of guidance. It is a GPS for a Christian. It leads a believer to the purpose that God has ordained for them. You will not see the place God has for you unless you obey what He says to you. Consider the GPS you use on your phone. Imagine inputting an address to a place you do not know, and then ignoring every turn it asks you to make. Because you do not know where you are going, you do not have the ability to get there on your own. Neglecting the voice that knows how to get there will result in you getting further away from your desired destination. This is exactly what is happening to many upcoming leaders. They are called, but have not arrived, because they ignore the directions that God provides.

The Importance Of Place

One common theme in scripture is the concept of place. God is constantly expressing concern about where His people are. After God establishes relationships with His people, shortly thereafter, He looks into their establishment in places that ensure their personal comfort and His expanded dominion.

The earliest example of this is the garden of Eden. God created man, gave him a purpose, but realized purpose without placement is pointless. A farmer without land cannot cultivate. How could this man be fruitful and multiply without a place that provided him the space to do so? Genesis 2 shares that "The Lord God planted a garden eastward in Eden; and there he put the man whom he had formed" (Genesis 2:8). Pay close attention to the way this verse is written. First, God prepared the place, and then He brought Adam to the place. As His child, God has prepared designated places for you that He wants to bring you into. Until you get to your assigned place, you will be unable to complete the assignment you were created for.

Too many people are only concerned about getting a title, but that is not enough for you to exercise power. You can be given a title, but it only matters in a place where you have jurisdiction. Consider a manager; reprimanding employees who violate company policy is one of their responsibilities. If you are a manager at a fast-food restaurant, you cannot reprimand a nurse in a hospital for misconduct. Although you have the title, being out of place disqualifies you from using the authority your title gives you. Think of a shark out of water. A ferocious, frightful fin can quickly become harmless and helpless outside of its proper environment. You have power and authority as a Joshua personality, but it is null and void if you are in the wrong place.

Recall that God is NOT a respecter of persons. In the same way that God prepared a place for Adam, God prepared a place for you. Jesus reveals this when He informs the disciples, "I go to prepare a place for you" (John 14:2). This was a prophecy of Heaven, as He refers to that same place as His "Father's house". Scriptures clearly demonstrate that the Father's house is in Heaven such as when the Prophet Isaiah refers to Heaven as God's throne (Isaiah 66:1). Jesus prepared a place for you in Heaven. You do not have to wait until you die to experience the benefits of that place. There are many believers who miss the ability to exercise power on Earth because they think the promises of salvation are only found after death. That is a major part of salvation, but it is not the only part. If God desired us to experience Heaven only when we die, He would not have created a man on Earth. Similarly, He would not have come to Earth and demonstrated how we ought to conduct ourselves while we are here if He did not want us here. He could have just made us in Heaven and kept us there. However, He told us to "occupy till I come" (Luke 19:13). It is difficult to properly occupy something when you don't understand the purpose of its creation.

Before we can further explain the importance of being in the right place, we must clarify that places have distinct purposes themselves. Consider everywhere you went today. Each of those places has an assignment attached to them. A bank is assigned to finance. A restaurant is assigned to feed. A government is assigned to govern. Earth is a place with a commission! Earth was not created for Heaven's restraint, but for Heaven's expansion. The Bible is not about a religion that worships a deity, but it is a constitution that relays the desires of the

King. The Bible makes us aware of an order of government that God wants established. In the same way that governmental powers desire to expand their kingdoms to foreign lands, God desires to expand His Kingdom to Earth. Earth is a colony of Heaven. This means that you do NOT have to wait until you die to go to Heaven to experience it! In Matthew 6, when Jesus was teaching His disciples how to pray, He requested that God's will be done "on Earth as it is in Heaven" (Matthew 6:10). No foreign government colonizes another county and changes its image to match that new country. This is why French is spoken in Haiti and Spanish in South America. When a foreign government takes over a territory, they impose their culture. Heaven is waiting to impose itself on us right now, not just when we die. To see a direct biblical comparison of Heaven to life on Earth as a believer, review 2 Corinthians 5:17 and Revelation 21:1-4.

Heaven's Embassy

Now that you understand Heaven is a Kingdom, we continue by emphasizing that a Christian is a citizen of the Kingdom of God. That is your first allegiance. When countries expand into other territories, they set up an embassy. For example, an ambassador of China can have an embassy in America. According to international law, when anybody visits the Chinese embassy in America, they are no longer on American soil. Since the embassy belongs to China, the embassy is on Chinese soil despite its physical location in the United States. The embassy is in two places at once. The embassy is in one place physically (the United States) but in another place unseen (China).

You are also a House! You are the temple of the Holy Spirit (1 Corinthians 6:19). In other words, you are an Embassy. Like the example of the Chinese embassy, you are in two places at once. You are on Earth physically, but you are elsewhere unseen. Can you take a guess where you are? Back in your home country. You are in Heaven! Recall when Jesus said, "I go to prepare a place for you" (John 14:1). So many believers think that He is getting Heaven ready. Heaven has already been created in the beginning (Genesis 1:1). So why would He be preparing something that He already established? The Greek word for "prepare" is Hetoimazo. When Kings were getting ready to travel, it is said that this word was used to describe the process in which they "made the roads passable"[1]. Prepare is not about the destination being ready, but the road to the destination being prepared. Therefore, when Jesus spoke of preparing a place, He meant the road to that place, or access to that place was being handled by Him. This is why He said, "I Go"! If Jesus did not GO to the cross, the veil would not have been split (Matthew 27:51); consequently, the access to the place would not be our portion. Because Jesus decided to GO, we are now able to GO! Look at what the prophet Isaiah shared when He prophesied about the ministry of Jesus, "I will go before you and level the uneven places; I will shatter the bronze doors and cut the iron bars in two." (Isaiah 45:2). This clearly demonstrates how the ministry of Jesus was all about giving people access to Heaven. The veil isn't ripped when we die, it is ripped as we speak, because He already decided to GO!

Not only did He go, but three days later, He returned for a purpose. Let's review what was said in John 14. Jesus shared, "In my Father's house are many mansions: if *it were* not *so*, I would have told you. I go to prepare a place for you. And if I go and prepare a place for you, I will come again, and receive you unto myself; that where I am, *there* ye may be also" (John 14:2-3). When He came back after resurrecting,

---

1. Recovered from https://www.biblestudytools.com/lexicons/gr eek/nas/hetoimazo.html

He gave us instructions on how to receive His spirit. In other words, He gave us the way to be where He is also, even while we are still on Earth. He gave us a representative at the table. To illustrate this, think of America's decision to elect representatives. Even though people from Miami do not go to Washington DC, they elect someone who has offices in both Miami and Washington to represent them where they cannot physically go. Although they are not in Washington, their elected official from the local community gives them a seat at the table. Because the Spirit of God is in Heaven and also in you, He gives you a seat at the table in Heaven. As a matter of fact, the Bible tells us specifically that we are "seated in Heavenly places" (Ephesians 2:6). I am on Earth, but I am merely an embassy. I am in one place physically, but spiritually, in the unseen, because I am the property of Heaven, I am on heavenly soil on Earth.

At least, I am supposed to be on Heavenly soil. Just because China has an embassy in America, that does not mean Chinese citizens are always in the embassy. The reality is, because of the temptation of the country that is hosting the embassy, Chinese citizens only visit their embassy when they have a need. Some reasons why citizens visit embassies are for "emergency passports, emergency protection, and when under arrest". Meaning, citizens don't go to embassies unless they are in a crisis where they are at a loss, limited, treated terribly, and/or in trouble. Isn't that the same for us? We can access Heaven via prayer at any time, but there is no need to call on our home country when our host country is giving us the time of our lives. We only seek Heaven when we are in trouble.

This became a reality for Adam and Eve. They had constant communication with Heaven. They stayed in the embassy. They were in the right spiritual place, but Eve decided to step out of communication with God. Eve decided to entertain communication with a resident of the host country, a snake that was cast down to Earth, named the Devil. He purposely placed distractions in the way of Adam and Eve to pull them away from the spiritual place that provided them with the guidance that sustained them physically. In the same way, social media, tv, relationships, and so many other things are distractions that the enemy uses to pull us out of our assigned spiritual place today. When you get out of the right place spiritually, in the presence of God through prayer, you end up losing the physical place God wanted you to occupy. Adam and Eve consequently got kicked out of the garden, and the same Earth they were put on to dominate ended up dominating them. In Eden, the trees provided for them. Out of Eden, they had to work like slaves for provision. If you are in the wrong place spiritually, you will ultimately be drawn out of the right place physically. Being in the wrong place physically makes it impossible to walk in purpose.

Joshua's entire ministry was dependent on a physical place. His responsibility was to lead God's people out of the wilderness into a promised land of milk and honey. As a young Joshua, make sure you clearly know your assignment. First, I am saying this because, if you walk in this type of calling, you might have a burning desire to save everybody. You cannot save everybody. God has over eight billion people on the planet and an alleged "one billion people" who profess to be Christians. You are physically unable to reach everyone. You are not the only one with an anointing. Various people have been empowered with different callings to perform a particular assignment. Stay in your lane and allow other anointed people to reach other arreas. Second, I am saying this to remind you that you are distinct. God deals personally with you. This means, your assignment will not look like someone else's. Just because you walk in an anointing similar to Joshua's does not mean your entire ministry assignment will be the same as Joshua's. Although Joshua took over for Moses, his assignment was not the same as Moses. While Moses was required to lead the children of Israel out of Egypt, Joshua only had to lead them into the Promised Land. Every Bible character has a specific assignment, including the Lord Jesus Christ. Jesus was sent only to Israel (Matthew 15:24). Paul wanted to go into Asia at a point of his ministry, but God did not allow him to do so at that time (Acts 16:6). Personally, I know I have been called to reach the youth and young adult population in and around Miami-Dade County. Depending on the season I am in, that specific assignment changes. Remembering what I have been assigned to do ensures I stay in the right place physically. For example, in 2022, as I was transitioning into college from high school, I desperately wanted to leave Miami. However, God did not allow me to leave. The school I applied to outside of Miami did not accept me despite my attractive application. As I reflect over my first year of college, that is the time where I have done the most successful ministry endeavors in Miami-Dade County. Imagine if I left the place God ordained for me to be. I would have missed the successes He already ordained for me to have in the place He assigned me to.

The bottom line is, place is important. If you are not in the right place, the purpose God has for you is unable to be executed. When God searched for Adam in the Garden, He asked the first ever question that appears in the Bible: "Where Are You?" (Genesis 3:7-15). I can not think of a greater piece of evidence to demonstrate that God is concerned about the places His people are in. It was not that Adam was no longer in Eden, but it was the fact that he hid himself. God did not hide from Adam. Adam hid from God. God never leaves nor forsakes a believer (Deuteronomy 31:8). Many people think that this means God will follow a believer wherever they go. Like David, they are convinced God will be with them if they make their bed in Hell

(Psalm 139:8). The reality is, while God is everywhere, His glory is not experienced everywhere. The world has His presence, but only the believers have His glory: His manifested, life-changing presence that we can feel and experience. Believers even miss out on His glory sometimes. The sins we commit cause separation between us and God. The guilt and shame make us drift from God (Isaiah 59:2). Him being made known and demonstrating all of who He is does not occur everywhere. To experience God in that particular way, you have to be in the proper spiritual place. This is why an omnipresent God can sometimes feel absent. Have you ever asked God, "Where are you?". Consider looking for someone in a dark room. You may think they are absent even though they are in the room because it is difficult to see them in the dark. In the same way, God may be right there, but you feel like He isn't. This may be because the darkness of the spiritual place you are in blinds you from the ability to see Him. Joshua could not be like the rest of the children of Israel, who stayed on the ground to worship a golden calf while God was on the mountain. He had to go to the proper spiritual place. He had to ascend. The question arises: will you ascend into the proper spiritual place so you can experience the Shekinah Glory of God in your life? Moses didn't even dare to try to complete His assignment without the glory of God (reference Exodus 33:18-23). Why would you dare to do your assignment without it? Let's go up and experience the glory of the Lord.

5

WHY DO I NOT UNDERSTAND?

I want you to recall what a mountain looks like. If you have never seen one before, take a moment to research one on the internet. Knowing what a mountain looks like is critical to your comprehension of this chapter. In reality, unless you have a familiarity with particular symbols, you will have trouble understanding the Bible. Like any other book, the Bible requires critical thinking and symbolic interpretation to fully grasp the message that God is trying to convey.

Parables: The Reason I Must Know Symbols

Have you ever read the Bible and wondered, "Why is this book so complicated?" Especially for all those who read the King James Version, I know there have been moments where you ask yourself, "Why is there so much use of figurative language?" If Jesus desired as many people as possible to become aware of the gospel, why was He not straightforward? Why did He speak in parables and answer the Pharisees with responses that leave us confused as we read? The disciples asked Jesus these questions in Matthew 13.

Matthew 13

10 *And the disciples came, and said unto him, Why speakest thou unto them in parables?* **11** *He answered and said unto them, Because it is given unto you to know the mysteries of the kingdom of heaven, but to them it is not given.*

I want us to closely examine some verses from this chapter of the Bible. First, pay attention to the use of the word "them". The disciples did not say, "Why do you speak to us in parables", but "Why do you speak to them?". The use of this language indicates that Jesus had two different ways of communicating. Clearer speech was meant for His followers. His figurative language was intended for those who did not diligently pursue Him the way His disciples did. God is serious about His Kingdom. This means while everyone is invited, every state of mind is not tolerated. People have a false theology that Jesus told people to "Come as you are", but there are not any scriptures that support Jesus articulating that sentiment. Jesus invited any and every one (who was a child of Israel during his time and all people now) into fellowship with Him, no matter their current state, but put a demand on them to "repent" when He called them. Jesus' entire message was centered around the word "repent" (Matthew 4:17). Repenting indicates turning in a different direction. When Jesus called people, they had to change their minds about what they currently were doing. Many of the disciples He called had occupations, but the Bible records them "forsaking" what they were doing to follow Him (Luke 5:11). The same thing remains true today. Salvation is free, but everything else is costly. Jesus wants everyone; however, those who are willing to sacrifice are the ones who receive the most from Him. His disciples got the most from Him because they sacrificed. Jesus does not cast "pearls before swine" (Matthew 7:6). Unless you indicate you have the desire and capacity for something, you will not receive it from God. Because the disciples made sacrifices to follow Jesus, they demonstrated that they were the type of people Jesus wanted to give mysteries to. Before we continue with Matthew 13, I want to show you two scriptures in Matthew 5 and Matthew 8.

Matthew 5

1 *And seeing the multitudes, he went up into a mountain: and when he was set, his disciples came unto him:* **2** And he opened his mouth, and taught them, saying,

Matthew 8

1 *When he was come down from the mountain, great multitudes followed him.*

These two scriptures show what happened before and after the sermon on the Mount. This is Jesus' first ever teaching. He began to explain His principles in order to establish His Kingdom on Earth. This sermon was similar to a constitution. Reading these two verses, I asked myself, "Why did Jesus go up on a *mountain* before doing His sermon?". In response to my question, God told me to recognize the size of the audience on the mountain compared to the size of the audience on the ground. On the ground, there are great multitudes, whereas, on the mountain there were only His few disciples. This means *hundreds to thousands* were willing to see Jesus on the ground, but only a *handful* of disciples (could be twelve or seventy) were willing to sacrifice to continue with Jesus in uncomfortable places.

You will find Jesus having a lot of dynamic encounters with people on Mountains. In Mark, He called the twelve disciples on a mountain and "ordained" them as Apostles (Mark 3:13). In Matthew, He called three of the disciples for a divine encounter called the Transfiguration, where He engaged Heaven on Earth (Matthew 17:2). Mountains tend to be a place where Jesus escaped the crowd. Jesus is not interested in the crowd. He is looking for those like the woman with the issue of blood who want to touch the hem of His garment (Luke 8:43-48). He is looking for those like Zacchaeus who are willing to climb trees to get His attention (Luke 19:1-10). Do you stand out in the midst of a crowd?

Mountain Climbers Stand Out In Crowds

Mountain climbing is not only a New Testament activity. Jesus was replicating a pattern God established with His people in the book of Exodus. In Exodus 19, you will find God put His presence in a mountain called Sinai. He requested all the children of Israel to come in the presence of the mountain to meet with Him. However, because of their fear, they rejected meeting with God and hearing from Him directly. Instead, they asked Moses to be their middleman. We should not judge the children of Israel because we have all done the same thing. Instead of seeking God ourselves sometimes, we look to a prophet or a pastor to tell us what God is saying. In reality, from the creation of man to His request of the children of Israel in Exodus 19, God has always wanted direct communication with His people. You do not have to wait for a prophet or a pastor because He wants to talk directly to you (see Hebrews 1:1-2). However, God only talks to those that want to hear Him.

God describes Himself as a jealous God (Exodus 34:14). He does not want to share your attention. The Mountain is a way to distinguish those who truly want Him from those who *pretend* they do. In the same way the disciples forsook their careers to see Jesus, climbing a mountain indicates sacrifice. You only make sacrifices for something you consider more valuable than the thing you are giving up. In today's age with modern technology, going up a mountain is already challenging. Consider driving up a gigantic mountain in the Caribbean with somewhat developed roads and plenty of potholes. That is not simple. Now, were there cars during biblical days? Were there construction workers to lay down the asphalt? The likelihood is everyone who climbed a mountain in Bible days did it by foot. They did not have the fancy roads we have now. This means if you decided to climb a mountain to meet God, it was an extreme sacrifice. Even today, I still don't understand why some people hike mountains. I personally would not like to make such a physical sacrifice. Therefore, I cannot blame people in the Bible for deciding to wait until Jesus came back down from the mountain to speak to Him. It is not easy to make these types of sacrifices.

Special Rewards For Mountain Climbers

Now that we can conceptualize the difficulty of climbing a mountain to meet God, we see why Jesus reserved special revelation for mountain climbers. Those who climbed mountains showed Jesus that they were not pigs (Matthew 7:6). They did not just eat anything without understanding the importance of what they were consuming. Instead, they were people who desperately wanted to know more.

They were okay with physically depriving themselves to receive more. While we emphasize the Kingdom of God, we must understand that Jesus was not the first person to preach about it. As a matter of fact, the Kingdom of God was prophesied in the Old Testament under a different name: Mount Zion. According to Isaiah 2, "It shall come to pass in the last days, that the mountain of the Lord's house shall be established in the top of the mountains, and shall be exalted above the hills; and all nations shall flow unto it." Isaiah 2 is a Messianic prophecy (prophecy about the Messiah) of the Kingdom that Jesus was coming to establish. The Bible wants people to understand that to meet God, you have to be in a particular place. You must go up in the mountain because that is where God is. He is not going to manifest himself to everyone on the ground, but to those who make the sacrifice to see Him where He is.

Don't Climb Mount Everest

In John 4, Jesus was ministering to the Woman at the Well. She was a Samaritan (a half jew). At that time, the Jews and Samaritans were divided because of their different races and theological beliefs. She knew the scriptures, but she took them too literally. Evidence of this is seen in the verses shared below that reference part of their conversation.

John 4

19 *The woman saith unto him, Sir, I perceive that thou art a prophet.* **20** *Our **fathers worshipped in this mountain; and ye say, that in Jerusalem is the place where men ought to worship**. 21 Jesus saith unto her, Woman, believe me, the hour cometh, when ye shall neither in this mountain, nor yet at Jerusalem, worship the Father.* **22** *Ye worship ye know not what: we know what we worship: for salvation is of the Jews.*

23 *But the hour cometh, and now is,* **when the true worshippers shall worship the Father in spirit and in truth:** *for the Father seeketh such to worship him.*

The woman understood that God preferred mountain top experiences, but she got too caught up with the physical place. Children of God do this all the time. They see principles of God and make them too literal when God utilized certain symbols to have a spiritual meaning. I am not telling you to climb the nearest mountain to pray. You can pray anywhere. However, when you position yourself to pray, it must be similar to the symbolism of climbing a mountain. You should be okay with leaving people behind and letting go of baggage to see Christ.

In reference to this, the psalmist asked the question, "Who may ascend the mountain of the Lord? Who may stand in his holy place? The one who has clean hands and a pure heart, who has not appealed to what is false, and who has not sworn deceitfully" (Psalm 24:3-4). Think of climbing a physical mountain one more time. As you climb that mountain, gravity is at work. It is attempting to pull you down. The more weight you have, the more gravity is working against you. For this reason, those who hike tend to pack light and leave unnecessary things on the ground. To see God, you cannot bring everyone and everything. You have to clean your hands and purify your heart. You must be like the disciples and forsake everything, just so you can ensure that you reach the spiritual mountain that God is asking you to climb.

The Reward Of The Mountain Is Understanding

At this point, you should understand that the mountain represents sacrificing to get in the *presence of God*. When the multitudes stayed on the ground and waited until Jesus came back down, they neglected His presence. On the other hand, the disciples prioritized His presence. Is His presence your priority or merely the place that you go to in an emergency? Do not pursue everything else and forsake getting in His presence. The Bible commands us to, "Seek ye first the Kingdom of God and His righteousness and all these things shall be added unto you" (Matthew 6:33). Now we will demonstrate how getting in the presence of God and seeking His face is a place where "addition" occurs. Let's return to the part of Matthew 13 that we were reading previously.

Matthew 13

12 *For whosoever hath, to him shall be given, and he shall have more abundance: but whosoever hath not, from him shall be taken away even that he hath.* **13** *Therefore speak I to them in parables: because they seeing see not; and hearing they hear not, neither do they understand.*

As mentioned before, the presence of God is a place where addition occurs. In verse 12, Jesus explains that those who have His presence will get more from it. On the contrary, those who do not have His presence (or do not make the climb up the mountain), will lose the very words Jesus already gave them. Did you know that it is possible to lose the word of God? Matthew 13 shares that those who hear the word, *but do not understand it*, will have that word stolen by the enemy (Matthew 13:19). This is why verse 13 of the passage says, they're seeing but "see not". Have you ever looked at something without your glasses? Although you are looking in the right direction, the lack of a proper instrument causes you to see a distorted image. As a result, you are unable to understand what you are seeing. The same goes for those who hear but "hear not". Imagine someone hard of hearing trying to understand without a hearing aid. They may hear a noise but miss the message because they did not have the proper instrument. The same thing goes for the teachings of Jesus. We have access to everything He is saying, but a failure to climb the mountain and access the tools of His presence will result in us not understanding. A word we do not understand is a word that the devil steals.

The Holy Spirit is the tool that helps us understand. He is our pair of glasses and our hearing aid. Imagine someone speaking to you in a foreign language. You may hear what they say, but you will need a translator to interpret for you. The Holy Spirit is the translator. He is one who both understands what Heaven is saying and what you are thinking. He will translate what God is saying to you in a way that you will comprehend. Among the many benefits of the presence of God, the greatest of these is understanding. Unless we engage with the Holy Spirit in the presence of God, we will not receive clarity. The reason why the Holy Spirit is known as the one who "teaches us all things" is because He breaks down the parts of God that are confusing for us (John 14:26). Look at what the Bible shares with us about comprehending spiritual things, "But the person without the Spirit does not receive what comes from God's Spirit, because it is foolishness to him; he is not able to understand it since it is evaluated spiritually" (1 Corinthians 2:14). How can we try to understand God without His Spirit? How do we engage with the Spirit without His Presence?

Understanding The Assignment

In the first chapter of this book, we looked at the call of Joshua to "Now, therefore arise". Revisit the entire chapter of Joshua 1. As you read it, you will find that Joshua received what I like to call a "download from God". Joshua had an encounter with God that detailed his assignment on the Earth. In the previous chapter, I emphasized the need to "know your assignment". The key to accomplishing that is climbing the mountain. When Joshua got in the presence of God, God clearly explained what he was put on Earth to do. Recall when Jesus called His disciples and ordained them as apostles in Matthew 10. That entire chapter is a clear explanation from Jesus of their assignment. If you do not know what you are called to do on the Earth, it may be a result of you failing to climb the mountain. If you received the assignment before, but have grown forgetful or discouraged, it could be because you have not climbed the mountain in a long time. For people like Abraham and Moses, God constantly reiterated the assignment. He reminded them of their purpose over and over during different points in their lives. This is not a one-time encounter, but a continuous lifestyle. God is closer to man than ever before. In the Old Testament, He was on a physical mountain. He could only be reached via a prophet. Today, He lives in the believer and could be reached anytime. What is your excuse? The Bible shares that the enemy does not have any time to waste (Revelation 12:17). Why do you? If you do not know at all, get in His presence, and get an understanding of your assignment. If you already know, get in His presence, and get the next steps and encouragement needed to continue the assignment.

6

WHO ARE YOU AROUND?

The first five chapters of this book are aimed to get you to your assignment. This chapter is a shift. As we move forward, we will focus on how to overcome the obstacles that are a threat to your assignment. In the last chapter, we learned that Joshua was finally released to take Moses' place. It is delusional to think that a release is freedom from any difficulty. Consider when a prisoner is released from their sentence. In the American restorative justice system, they are still faced with several challenges. It is difficult for them to get jobs. Based on the conditions of their parole, some of them can not go to certain places or be around certain people. There are obstacles that try to hold them back despite their releasement. The same happens when you are released on your assignment. There will be obstacles attempting to hold you back. These obstacles are constant. I did not see these challenges coming on my own faith journey, so I wrote this book to warn you about them. I do not want you to be blind sighted the way I was. Take heed to everything we discuss from this point forward, because there is a strong likelihood you will come across similar difficulties if you have not already.

You Are A Threat, Even If You Did Not Start Yet

The first set of challenges you will come across are what I consider "premature" obstacles. This is opposition that comes against you before you even start your kingdom assignment. Some actually come across it before they even know their assignment. One may ask, "Why does the enemy come against me when I have not even done anything yet?". This is because the enemy can be aware of your purpose before you are even familiar of it. He will try to kill the seed before it gets a chance to take root.

Everything that God wants to do is spoken before it is manifested. Consider how God created the world in Genesis 1. He said let there be and there was. In reference to this, the book of Hebrews shares that, "the worlds were framed by the word of God" (Hebrews 11:3). Everything we experience is a by-product of His word. The word may not happen instantaneously; however, it eventually happens in spite of how long it takes (Habbakuk 2:3-4).The same thing is true about your calling. God has been speaking over you ever since He created you. There are words from God for an appointed time concerning your destiny. Just because you did not hear it does not mean He never said it. Even when you miss it, the devil is always paying attention. His goal is to challenge what God said. He challenged the word that the Father spoke over Jesus. In Matthew 3, the Father proclaimed,"This is My Beloved son, in whom I'm well pleased" (Matthew 3:17). In Matthew 4, the devil requested of Jesus to prove if He is really the son of God

(Matthew 4:6). In the same way, the Devil desires to challenge every word God has spoken over you.

The entire Old Testament testifying of Jesus is an example of how God speaks over us far before our arrival. The earliest prophecy of Jesus is found in the book of Genesis (Genesis 3:15). Abraham even received a prophecy about Jesus (Genesis 22:14). A majority of all the prophetic books (Isaiah-Malachi), especially Isaiah, give detailed aspects about what the calling and characteristics of Jesus will entail. This means when Jesus was born, the spiritual realm was already familiar with who He was. For this reason, the enemy tried to kill Him as a baby. In Matthew 2, you will find that the wise men already knew that Jesus was a King at his birth. This is because of the prophecies spoken about him (Matthew 2:5). In response to this, King Herod, the ruler at the time, issued a decree to kill every boy in the land under the age of two to stop Jesus from living (Matthew 2:16). The enemy was desperate to stop Jesus' purpose before He became physically able to manifest it. Jesus shared that, "If they persecuted me, they will also persecute you" (John 15:20). We are not exempt from being targeted by the enemy before we are physically able to walk in our calling. As we move forward in this book, we will locate the vulnerable areas in our lives that the Devil seeks to attack.

Your Relationships Are A Target

Whether you are an introvert who enjoys solitude or an extrovert who is the life of the party, the enemy can use your social preference as an open door for him to attack you. Relationships in and of themselves are not bad. As a matter of fact, godly relationships are a threat to the enemy. After calling everything He made good, the first time God said, "it is not good" was in reference to man being alone (Genesis 2:18).

Recall that man was made in the image of God. **That means we are a reflection of the way God is structured.** One aspect of God is that He is a family. Evidence of this is seen when the Bible states that "God said, Let *US* make man" (Genesis 1:26). God is not one person. He is three persons who are one God. Let it be made clear that God is not three parts, but three persons. Each person is God, with all of God. They make up the God family. God the Father, God the Son (also known as the Word per John 1:1,14), and God the Spirit. John elaborates on this by sharing that, "For there are three that bear record in heaven, the Father, the Word, and the Holy Ghost: and these three are one" (1 John 5:7). Therefore, even God did not choose solitude. He decided to have company.

Jesus was not even a lone ranger when He left heaven. If anybody did not need anybody, it was God himself on the Earth. Making a decision to be all by yourself with nobody else is unbiblical. Scripture emphasizes the power in unity. Ecclesiastes 4:9-12 elaborates on the beauty of "two being better than one" (Ecclesiastes 4:9). Through the divine help of God, the Bible shares it is possible for one to chase 1000 and two to put 10000 to flight (Deuteronomy 32:30). For this reason, Jesus decided to have 12 disciples on the journey with Him. When He wanted to do certain miracles such as the healing of Jarius' daughter, He made sure to carry His inner circle of three friends: Peter, James, and John (Mark 5:37). These three men went on to be unapologetic defenders and Fathers of the Faith. If Jesus was not too good for community, what makes you think you are?

The Enemy Loves You Isolated

Many are familiar with the story of the prophet Elijah. This mighty man of God went on to kill hundreds of prophets of Baal in 1 Kings

18. By the next chapter, his boldness disappeared as he ran away in fear of a death threat. As you read his story in 1 Kings 19, you will find that he became a suicidal, emotional wreck. One key verse I want to point out in that chapter is, "And when he saw that, he arose, and went for his life, and came to Beersheba, which belongeth to Judah, and *left his servant there*" (1 Kings 19:3). Elijah had a right-hand man named Elisha who went with him everywhere. However, during his time of fear and pain, he went into isolation. He did not permit his servant to join him.

As young leaders, we tend to be strong for everyone else, but neglect receiving that same help in return. I recall being there for many of my peers during their tears and tribulations, but being unable to call any of them during mine. It is easy to blame them and claim they were unavailable; however, the reality was I did not request for help. Because of my position as the "youth leader", I was too prideful to acknowledge that I needed help. I was ashamed. I did not want to appear as if I was weak. This is a foolish way of thinking. This is a strategy of the enemy designed to make you relinquish your destiny. The devil understands you will be unable to make it unless you have people around you. Consider Jesus anxiously praying in the garden of Gethsemane in Matthew 26. He took His inner circle of 3 (Peter James, and John) to be with Him. This was the weakest He ever was. Recall, they received a revelation that He was God (the Christ, the anointed Son from God in Matthew 16:16-17). He could have been afraid of their perspective of Him. How could He claim to be God yet be so anxious? The reality is, no human is beyond calamity that produces anxiety. **You do not have to be a superhuman.** If you visit Matthew 26, you will find that the disciples were sleeping during His time of prayer. I believe this symbolically represents that they were not even paying attention to His weaknesses. True community given to you by God will minimize their attention on your errors and magnify their encouragement during your time of weakness. Find yourself a community. Now that you know you need relationships, you have to ensure you choose the correct ones. The enemy's desire is to make sure you don't.

1. Choose Healthy Spiritual Leaders

I wish that every person that claimed to be from God was truly of God, but that is not the case. The Bible warns that there will be many false prophets (Matthew 7:15); consequently, everybody who wears the Jesus jersey may not play by His rules. Experiences with false spiritual leaders may be the reason why people do not go to church in the first place. You cannot feed into this trap by the enemy. The failure to have the proper christian community will play a role in deterring your destiny.

Joshua had Moses. Without Moses, Joshua would not be able to walk in destiny. First and foremost, Moses' ministry was critical to the release of Joshua from slavery. Their ministry was setting Joshua up far before he even considered being a minister. Proper spiritual leaders will have the eye-sight and insight to get you out of spiritual bondage and set you up for future successes. As for me, my Apostle Errol and Pastor Angela Williams have been pastoring New Alpha Worship Center for over 20 years. If it was not for their church, I would not have met Jesus Christ. I would still be under the spiritual bondage of the enemy. Their ministry aided in my release. This process continues. Moses constantly interceded for the Israelites to be spared from God's wrath (Exodus 32:11). This means Mosesbconsistently aided in Joshua overcoming demise. In times of suicidal ideation, depression, grief due to the loss of family members, and fatigue, my leaders had no problem showing up to my door step to hug me and pray with my family and I. They are what the Bible describes as pastors after God's own heart (Jeremiah 3:15). Secondly, their drive to start their ministry is what made my ministry so much easier. I practiced preaching on their pulpit and doing miracles on their altar. I practiced public speaking on their radio station. They are so humble. They don't even consider any of these things as their own belongings. They consider themselves stewards of God's belongings with a mandate to use them for advancement of others. Pastor Ron Harper, a friend of theirs, shared a revelation that God gives leaders "power to empower".

As a young leader, you need a leader similar to Moses. One that pushes you forward and has your back. This is seen in Exodus 17 when Moses held up the rod (which represents intercession and covering) while Joshua fought on the ground. David was not as fortunate. He had a leader who grew jealous of him and held him back. Saul did not like David once he started to garner more attention. The Bible records Saul demoting David, and even trying to kill him (1 Samuel 18:11-13). Just because you have a Saul, I am not instructing you to leave immediately. Pray and ask God for guidance on the Mountain. If He gives you permission to leave, pray and discern for a leader who wants to build your gifts, not a leader who wants to use you to build their own name.

2. Choose Healthy Spiritual Friends

As a young leader, you need somebody to commune with and talk to. However, that does not mean you go around telling everybody what you are going through. Even though someone is godly, that may not be the godly person assigned to you. The reality is, not everybody has a good heart. While some listen to your problems and try to be a source of encouragement, others get in your business to accumulate ammunition against you. Jesus did not take His twelve disciples everywhere, but He had a select three. Get you a select one or two to stick beside you. Through discernment by the Spirit, Jesus kept Judas close but not in His inner circle. Pray and ask God about the friends you have, because they will either be what a wise prophetess in my church called a "purpose pusher" or a "placeholder". This means that they will push you into your calling or take up unnecessary space in your life.

Recall the words of Apostle Paul, "Be not deceived: evil communications corrupt good manners" (1 Corinthians 15:33). Many people translate this to, "Bad company corrupts good morals" (1 Corinthians 15:33 CSB). The most heartbreaking thing for me is seeing someone, who recently experienced salvation, falling back into the world because they selected the wrong friends. You are a product of your environment. If you want to quit doing a certain sin, you cannot surround yourself with people who carelessly enjoy that offense. If you want to stop cursing, remove yourself from those with filthy mouths. If you want to stop lusting, remove yourself from those who are lustfully minded. The same goes for any other sin you want to stop doing. If you do not remove yourself from them, they will constantly keep pulling you into what they do. This verse also applies to Christian friends. Many people think this verse is only for worldly people; however, the King James translation does not even refer to the quality of the person. Instead, it refers to the quality of their speech. It shares that "evil communication" is the toxin. If you have a "God fearing friend" who does not speak life into you, they do not need to be around you. The reality is, most people who claim to be christian do nothing but gossip. This is an example of evil communication that corrupts your destiny. Recall all the time you spent gossiping. Imagine how different your faith would be if you used that same time to pray or have biblical discussion. It is not enough to have a christian friend. Do you have godly conversations with that friend? Look at what Paul instructed us, "Let no corrupt communication proceed out of your mouth, but that which is good to the use of edifying, that it may minister grace unto the hearers" (Ephesians 4:29). Rid yourself from conversations that do not build you.

Lastly, whoever is around you has your ear. Whoever has your ear will have your faith. Look at what Paul explains, "So then faith cometh by hearing, and hearing by the word of God" (Romans 10:17). Whatever you hear is whatever you have faith in. If you hear lies, you will believe lies. This means that Christians should be trying to hear what God is saying in everything they listen to. This is the only way we fortify ourselves from the discouragement of the enemy. Do your friends hold your arms up like Aaron and Hur did to Moses in Exodus 17? Do they speak the word of God to keep you going, or do they discourage you from believing? What type of friend are you? Do you encourage or discourage? The Bible is the founder of the golden rule, which shares that you will receive whatever you give (Luke 6:38). Maybe it is difficult for you to attract good friends because you have not been the type of friend that you desire to have.

Being in this position taught me to keep my mouth shut. Because young Joshuas tend to be biblically informed, they can ignorantly assume that they are always spiritually right. Concerning the lives of my friends, I always knew a bible story similar to their calamity. I used that as a license to speak over their destiny. The reality is, God was not requiring me to say anything at all. Even when they asked me for advice, I had to learn to say "I do not have anything to say" in moments where I did not hear God speak to me about their situation. We have to be spirit led in everything that we do, because saying the wrong thing could greatly affect someone's life. This was the case of Job's friends. The entire book of Job is a back and forth between Job and his friends. His friends were convinced that Job's sin caused his calamity, but that was far from the case. Their words caused more stress in Job's life when they were supposed to encourage him during his season of difficulty. It is not that they were biblically inaccurate, but they were spiritually out of order. They said biblical words that God did not grant them permission to say at that time. Intend to be a friend who only speaks when God asks you to. Have friends who speak what God says when God gives them permission to. As a person who reads the Bible and hears God on the mountain, you should discern and ask God to confirm every word anybody speaks to you, regardless of their position or title.

3. Wait On Romantic Relationships

From my personal observation, I have found that many new believers pursue a romantic relationship right after meeting Christ. A majority of the believers in my midst, who experienced salvation or rededication, pursued relationships shortly thereafter. I believe this is a strategy of Satan. Romantic relationships are not always demonic but they can be enormous distractions. For this reason, Paul wanted to emphasize the beauty of singleness to the church in Corinth. He warned them that, "I want you to be without concerns. The unmarried man is concerned about the things of the Lord—how he may please the Lord. But the married man is concerned about the things of the world—how he may please his wife— and his interests are divided. The unmarried woman or virgin is concerned about the things of the Lord, so that she may be holy both in body and in spirit. But the married woman is concerned about the things of the world—how she may please her husband" (1 Corinthians 7:32-34 CSB). Paul wanted to emphasize that a romantic relationship has the ability to pull a believer from God, if they do not have the discipline to set their priorities in order.

The elephant in the room must be addressed. If you have been in the Kingdom of God for a while, you can think of young leaders who were on fire. Eventually, there are plenty of them who lost it after dating a person. I warned you to choose healthy spiritual leaders and choose healthy friends; however, I feel led to instruct you to **wait on a romantic relationship**. The book of Ecclessiastes repeats the following, "Young women of Jerusalem, I charge you, do not stir up or awaken love until the appropriate time" (Song of Solomon 8:4). I am not suggesting that you be lonely forever, but I am saying that there is an appropriate time. There is a time when you will meet the person you are supposed to be with. Do not rush to be with any person. The wrong person, or even the right person at the wrong time, could be a threat to your destiny. Sometimes, this is an area in my life I wish I could do over. Nonetheless, I learned that there is no condemnation in Christ (Romans 8:1). The mistakes I committed yesterday are not a factor in my worthiness of receiving my future. Christ already paid the price for me to receive all that He has planned for me, despite my mistakes and my errors.

4. Trust God With Your Family

I do not know what your relationship is with your parents, siblings, cousins, and more. While we are on the subject of relationships, I did not want to leave the only relationship you did not pick for yourself out. This is the relationship God assigned to you. You can not break up with your parents. You can not cut off your siblings. As much as you try to separate from them emotionally, you are still connected to them genetically. Why did God give us such permanent bonds? It could be one of three reasons. First, God might have supplied you with a loving and supportive family to help you walk in your purpose. This is the case of my mother, Ingrid Cruickshank, and my siblings George and Nikki. Without them, I would not have been able to walk in my destiny. They have been my everything. The enemy tries to magnify their bad over their good in an attempt to break me away from them, because he understands how beneficial my proximity to them is to my destiny. Don't let the enemy augment the mistakes of those who God uses to help you. When you are still feeling the pain of a string, your emotions tend to lead you to overreact to offenses. Young leaders cannot afford to overreact. A wrong decision is costly. Instead, you have to pray and ask God for healing. This ensures that you would not make emotional decisions that you did not truly mean. Second, you might have family members who are present, but currently divided. You might be surrounded by heated arguments and disagreements that cause disarray. This is an opportunity for you to grow in your spirituality. Any time we see a situation in our lives, we aren't supposed to run away from it. Instead, we are supposed to **run *with the word of God* towards it**. I encourage you to start praying for your family and your household. A scripture I recommend is, "Then my people will dwell in a peaceful place, in safe and secure dwellings" (Isaiah 32:18). Saying this scripture over my home transformed my family dynamic. Lastly, you may have a horrible relationship with your family for a number of different reasons. You may have an absent parent or an abusive relative. What if I told you, they are not that bad. Individuals like that also play a role in pushing you in your destiny. It is easy to focus on the beneficial people, but we serve a God that says "all things work together for good" (Romans 8:28). This includes the bad family members. How? Keep reading to find out more.

7

WHAT TIME IS IT?

As we transition into the next section of this book, I want to emphasize and describe two aspects of God:

1. God Does Not Change His Nature

The nature, or character, of God is not transient. As discussed in Chapter 4, the characteristics of God are consistent. They remain the same all over scripture. God will continue to be that way eternally. This is embodied in the scripture that shares, "He is the same yesterday, today, and forevermore" (Hebrews 13:8). For example, God did not become a God of grace in the New Testament only. From Genesis, He was extending grace to mankind. Similarly, God's fervor for righteousness did not retire when He instituted the dispensation of grace and did away with the dispensation of the law. The same way He demanded righteousness under the law, the expectation remains under grace.

2. God Does Change His Execution

While God remains the same, it does not mean that everything He does is similar. While the character, or moral qualities, of God remain the same, the way in which He expresses those consistent morals varies based on timing. For example, in the Old Testament, a relationship with God was given to the children of Israel only. In the New Testament, through the sacrifice of Christ and the ministry of Paul, a relationship with God was offered to all people. In the book of Isaiah, God described himself as doing a "new thing" (Isaiah 43:19). He went on to charge His people to "Remember ye not the former things, neither consider the things of old" (Isaiah 43:18). A failure to understand that God does things differently from the way He did them previously will cause one to miss what God is doing currently. Many believers reject a new thing because they expect God to do things the way He always has.

Spiritual Seasons

Many people misinterpret what God is doing because they are unaware of the season that they are in. A season is a unit of time that indicates a distinct set of qualities from another time. The winter season has a completely different set of qualities from the summer season. King Solomon informs us in scripture that, "To everything there is a season, and a time to every purpose under the heaven" (Ecclesiastes 3:1). In simple words, different things occur in varying seasons. It only snows in the winter. Winter also requires a different attire from the summer season. If you do not know what season you are in, you will be unable to properly adapt and participate in the next move of God that is occurring.

This became a concern for Jesus when dealing with the Pharisees. He rebuked them by saying, "O ye hypocrites, ye can discern the face of the sky; but can ye not discern the signs of the times?" (Matthew 16:3). Jesus scolded the Pharisees because they drifted from a principle that God emphasized with their forefathers. In the early days of the children of Israel, God gave certain tribes distinct functions. For example, the tribe of Judah was responsible for praise and kings (such as David). The tribe of Levi was responsible for the care of the tabernacle and priests (such as Aaron). God also gave a specific duty to the tribe of Issachar. It is revealed in the book of Chronicles that the men of Issachar, "Were men that had understanding of the times, to know what Israel ought to do" (1 Chronicles 12:32). The specific role of this tribe was to identify what season Israel was in or approaching. Jesus was disgruntled that the Pharisees dismissed this important quality that God instilled in their forefathers. Reason being, a failure to know the season will result in an inability to properly respond to it. You do not wear winter clothes in the summertime. Because you know the season, you prepare for it in order to be successful in it. If we do not know the spiritual time, or the season God has us in, we will be unprepared for it and respond incorrectly.

Over the course of the rest of this book, we will closely examine five spiritual seasons that I believe every Christian will come across during their faith journey. We will look at these seasons through the life of Joshua and Joseph. The five seasons are:

1. Promise

2. Privilege

3. Persecution

4. Postponement

5. Prosperity

The rest of this book will fully explain the nature of each spiritual season and how they relate to leadership.

Management Is Not Ownership

As a young leader, one of your roles is that of a visionary; more specifically, you are one who constantly sees what God desires on Earth in the realm of the Spirit. Leadership is not ownership. Leadership is management. When Saul was anointed to be King over the Children of Israel, Prophet Samuel explained to him that he was selected as a "Captain over the Lord's inheritance" (1 Samuel 10:1). A captain is simply a manager. In a fast-food restaurant, a manager does not have any real power to make changes. They do not have the liberty to alter the menu or create their own systems. Their responsibility is to simply execute the vision of the franchise owner. Similarly, as young leaders it must be understood that we are not doing whatever we want to do. Although we are in positions of power, we do not have the liberty to be self-willed. The people are not our people. Instead, we are managing people that belong to God. This is why God gives us vision. He has desires for His people that He wants executed, and our responsibility is to get a vision of those desires to make sure they are fulfilled. This is why people like Moses constantly climbed the mountain. He was getting vision from God so he could properly execute what God wanted for the children of Israel. It is very important that we do not try to be *dictators* as young leaders. Jesus made it clear that true biblical leaders understand servitude (Matthew 23:11). It is not about controlling others or building a name for yourself. If that is your goal, you are not ready for leadership. You need to go through a season of pruning. Leadership is all about serving God by serving the people you lead. Unless you follow God's exact instructions, you will not lead properly.

Kingdom Of Priests

If you closely read 1 Samuel 8, you will find that God did not desire for Israel to have a king like Saul. God only allowed them to have one because they deeply desired it despite His warnings that it would be harmful to them. Does this mean that God did not want us to have leaders? Absolutely not! Leadership is a God-ordained principle found all over the Bible from people like Moses and Joshua to modern day apostles, prophets, evangelists, pastors, and teachers. The thing is, Israel only wanted a king to be like other nations (1 Samuel 8:19-20). They wanted their king to reflect other kings from foreign nations. The kings of this world are not the type of kings God wanted us to have. When God delivered the children of Israel, He told them that, "Ye shall be unto me a Kingdom of Priests, and a Holy Nation" (Exodus 19:6). Holy simply means set apart. They would not be a reflection or copycat of other nations, but they will be distinct because of their difference in operation. While other nations selected a single king who ruled based on his own desires, Israel's Kingdom would be based on priests. A priest in scripture was someone who atoned for the sins of Israel. The symbol of the priest is intimacy and constant communion with God. It also represents the person who constantly wants to reconcile and be in right standing with God. God wanted us to be kings and rulers, but our dominance in the world is dependent on our devotion to Him. Since we are not like earthly kings, we cannot do it from our own will. We need to be "kings and priests" (Revelation 1:6). We are a "royal priesthood" (1 Peter 2:9). Therefore, in order for us to lead others and dominate on Earth, our priority should be that of the priest. We should be constantly climbing the mountain to connect with God, so we can hear from Him. If we do not prioritize devotion through that of a priest, we neglect the dominion God designed for us to have as a king. If we prioritize the priesthood by spending time with God, He will give us visions such as those of promise.

Season #1:Promise

A promise is the assurance that someone is going to do something. Promises are a major part of God's communication with His people. There are several examples in scripture where God made promises to people in their initial encounter with Him. This is the case of Joshua. In Joshua 1, when God started to speak to Joshua directly in Moses' stead, you will find that God made several promises to Joshua concerning his ministry. Before you start any assignment, you will go through a season of promise. God will give you a taste of where you are going spiritually before getting there physically. Evidence of this occurs when Abraham was allowed to walk in the promised land hundreds of years before Joshua led them into it (Genesis 13:17). There are four ways you can receive the promise:

1. **Audibly**: God will speak in a way where you hear Him. It might not be a voice in your ear, but a strong impression in your spirit. It is a heavy burden on your heart. The word of God should confirm that the promise is of God's nature. God does not speak outside of the premises in the Bible.

2. **Vision**: God will show you while you are awake.

3. **Dream**: God will show you while you are sleeping.

4. **Prophetically**: God will use a prophet to tell you. If you are prioritizing the priesthood and constantly communing with God, the prophet will come to mostly provide confirmation. They will come to reassure you of something that God already showed you. They should rarely give new information. We should not be dependent on prophetic voices to hear from God (Hebrews 1:1-2).

In order to properly navigate a season of promise, there are two things that must be understood:

1. God Wants To Speak To You About Your Future

Paul tells us that, "Eye hath not seen, nor ear heard, neither have entered into the heart of man, the things which God hath prepared for them that love him. But God hath *revealed them unto us* **by His Spirit**" (1 Corinthians 2:9-10). Because every believer has the spirit of God, every believer has the ability to hear from God (Galatians 3:2). You do not have to be a prophet to hear from God. As long as you have the Spirit of God, you have access to revelation from God. All you have to do is demonstrate you have a desire to hear and see. God notices this about you based on how deeply you pursue friendship with Him. In the same way you share the tea with your inner circle, God shares what He is doing with friends. Jesus told the disciples that, " I do not call you servants anymore, because a servant doesn't know what his master is doing. I have called you friends, because I have made known to you everything I have heard from my Father" (John 15:15 CSB). Do not disqualify yourself from hearing from God. Do not pursue a prophet, pursue His presence. He will speak to you and use a prophet to confirm it in His divine timing.

2. Promises Could Be Generationally Inherited

Joshua was not the first person to receive the promise he was given. Abraham was the original receptor of the promise. Moses also received the promise. The worst thing a young leader can do is neglect the insight of the older generation. One of the aspects of Joshua that qualified him to be a successful leader was the fact that he sat under the admonition of Moses' generation. This allowed him to garner the wisdom, insight, and experience necessary to lead Israel. Without knowing their history, he couldn't lead them to their destiny. How else would he know the promise? This is why the Bible constantly tells us to honor our parents and submit to elders (Ephesians 6:1, 1 Peter 5:5). Doing so will enable us to optimize time by learning from their experience instead of wasting time trying to figure it out on our own.

Some argue that it is better to neglect the former generation because they are flawed. The flaws of the Moses generation did not hinder Joshua's ministry. Instead, their flaws played a vital role in propelling Joshua's ministry. Maturing as a young leader involves realizing that corrupt leaders are also assigned by God. There are countless examples in scripture. First, the bad of a leader does not disqualify their good. Moses did not make it to the Promise Land; however, the training he gave Joshua for leadership was not in vain. Moses was still able to anoint Joshua as his replacement. Eli stopped honoring God concerning correcting his sons; on the other hand, the training he gave Samuel about hearing the voice of God was still beneficial despite his own unrighteousness (1 Samuel 3). Saul was jealous of David, but he was critical to David's growth as a soldier. Second, the hardships a leader puts you through is essential to purifying you. Lastly, the faults of the former generation can still train you by simply demonstrating what you should not do. When Moses struck the rock instead of speaking to it, he showed Joshua a mistake that should not continue in the next generation (Numbers 20). Whether your leaders are healthy or unhealthy, they are still God's anointed; therefore, you can still learn from them, and you must be very careful about what you do to them and say about them (Psalm 105:15).

The Time Of Promise Is NOT The Time Of Fulfillment. However, Fulfillment Is Guaranteed!

It took hundreds of years after the promise was given to Abraham for the children of Israel to actually possess the Promise Land. We are going to examine several reasons as to why it took so long for the promise to be fulfilled. You have to understand that this is a process. Just because it takes a long time to happen does not mean it will not happen at all. Habakkuk reminded us of this when he shared that, "the vision is yet for the appointed time; it testifies about the end and will not lie. Though it delays, wait for it, since it will certainly come and not be late" (Habakkuk 2:3 CSB). The enemy likes to cast doubt about the promise by emphasizing how long the process is. A lengthy process does not disqualify the promise. God is not a liar (Numbers 23:19). Everything He said will come to pass (Isaiah 55:11). Even if you do not live to see it like Abraham did not, there will be a time when it comes to pass eventually. Your job is to keep the faith. It is easy to believe when you just heard it, but as you navigate other seasons, the devil wants you to stop believing. The enemy understands your belief is essential to its fulfillment.

Keep The Faith

One of the reasons why Moses did not see the Promised Land was because He did not keep the faith. God told him that, "Because ye believed me not, to sanctify me in the eyes of the children of Israel, therefore ye shall not bring this congregation into the land which I have given them" (Numbers 20:12). Faith is needed for you to obey God as He moves you towards the promise. A lack of Faith will cause you to drift and eventually miss the fulfillment of the promise. "Faith without works is dead" (James 2:26). True Faith will result in obedience. If you do not move on the word He gave you when He tells you to move, you are not operating in faith. In order to keep the faith, you have to remind yourself of the word. The Bible shares that, "Faith cometh by hearing, and by hearing the Word of God" (Romans 10:17). Notice the syntax of this verse. It does not just say that faith comes by hearing the Word of God, but faith simply comes by *hearing* alone. Whatever you hear (whether it be the Word of God or the report of the enemy) will result in what you believe. Personally, I try to remind myself of the word in everything that I do. My friends speak the word. My music speaks the word. The promises God gave me are posted on the walls of my bedroom and the lock screen of my phone. I refuse to forget what God said! If I forget what I heard, I will also lose my faith.

Many people think that we fight against the devil. I disagree with that. Christ already defeated Him. The reality is, we fight for our faith that Christ gives us victory over the enemy. The work of Christ is a finished work. When He died, He proclaimed "It is Finished" (John 19:30). Everything we need from God is already ours. The question is: do we believe it? Paul shared that, "I have fought a good fight, I have finished my course, I have kept the faith" (2 Timothy 4:7). The armor of God is an entire armor that is meant to defend us from doubt. For example, the shield is of faith. More so, every other piece is a part connected to our faith. This includes the breastplate of righteousness and helmet of salvation. Righteousness and salvation are aspects that we need to believe in so we can receive the promises of God. We only believe based on what we hear. That is why we have shoes that are the gospel and a belt that is the truth. That is the word of God that we hear to keep the Faith. Lastly, the sword of the Spirit is the word itself. The only way we offensively attack the enemy is by using what God told us. When the Devil tries to tell us that we cannot be who God has called us to be, the promise of God (that is irrevocable), has the potency to push back the enemy's attacks. Fight for your faith, and it will fight against the enemy for you. Without faith, you will be unable to survive the next spiritual seasons.

8

WHAT DO YOU EXPECT?

I n this chapter, we will discuss two spiritual seasons: privilege and persecution.

Season #2: Privilege

Right after a season of promise, most children of God are met with a season of privilege. Privilege occurs when you experience special treatment or advantage compared to others around you. Christians are supposed to be privileged compared to those in the world; additionally, some christians are even privileged over other christians *in certain areas of their lives* for the glory of God. As a believer in Jesus, privilege is more than just a season. It is your permanent lifestyle despite whatever season you are in. A season of privilege is just a time where you experience special treatment in the absence of persecution. It also is the motivation that precedes a season of persecution.

Favor: It Feels Good To Be The Favorite

The nature of God involves kindness. For this reason, He favors His people. He shows them kindness in certain areas that they did not deserve. This privilege isn't merely for their personal satisfaction, but for His honor and glory. One young lady who received this was Esther. She was favored to become the King's wife over other women because God gave her that blessing for His honor and glory. Her becoming the Queen was not merely for her personal gratification. It was for God's magnification and the advancement of His will for His people. While favor is freely given by God, it is *received at a cost*. The cost of this is obedience to God and wise counsel. Chapter 4 emphasized that, "What He says is a GPS". While favor and privilege is a destination that God wants you to access, you will be required to follow His voice in order to reach that place. Proverbs tells us that once you prioritize obeying God and remaining faithful, "Then you will find favor and high regard with God and people" (Proverbs 3:4 CSB). Esther did not have to impress the King or do extra actions to grab his attention, she just listened to God and Mordecai (her spiritual leader). As a result, she experienced the privilege. To elaborate on the privilege in the life of Joshua, we are going to examine his former generations through the life of Joseph and the children of Israel in Exodus.

I Did Not Ask For This!

Joseph received favor from his father for reasons that he could not control. It was because of who his mother was (Genesis 37:2). Because of this favor, he received special treatment that he did not even ask for. In the same way, the children of Israel received favor for reasons that they could not control. It was because of who their Father was. They were not only Abraham's children of promise, but God's chosen children that he **handpicked to manifest His glory through**. As a result of this favor, the children of Egypt testified that "the people of the children of Israel are more and mightier than we" (Exodus 1:9). The children of Israel did not ask for this kind of treatment. God gave it to them for reasons beyond their control. It was not only for their personal satisfaction, but it was divinely orchestrated by God for the glory of Himself. I can personally testify of receiving benefits that others did not experience for reasons beyond my control. God just favored me, and I pray He continues to do so.

Be Careful What You Ask For!

As I ask for more favor, I have to be reminded that the favor is for an assignment. Pastor Travis Greene once said, "God does not open doors for man, but God opens doors for God"[1] . Before you pray and ask God for favor, do not forget that the favor is for His glory. If you do not want to reveal His glory, you are not a candidate for His favor. To add, before you declare yourself as someone who wants to reveal His glory, you must know how glory comes. Glory is compared to new wine and fresh oil in scripture (Joel 2:19). Grapes are crushed to produce wine. Olives are pulverized to produce oil. If you request privilege from God, you must be ready to push past the pain needed to produce it.

---

1. Pastor Travis Greene: Cuffed to Construction. Sermon on Youtube by Transformation Church.

Privilege Invites Persecution

The seasons of Privilege that Joseph and the Children of Israel experienced were short lived. Those seasons expired when persecution became their portion. Children of God go through two types of painful seasons: persecution and postponement. The difference between these two seasons is based on their sources. The devil is the source of persecution, but you are the source of postponement. For Joseph, Genesis 37 lets us know that his brothers became extremely jealous of him. They desired to kill him because of the favor he received from his father. Similarly, the children of Israel were put into slavery because of the favor God allowed them to experience. Because the enemy hates your privilege, his priority is your expiration. He will put anything in your way to ensure you are limited. He wants to stop you from giving birth to what God has impregnated you with.

Season #3:Persecution

Our next topic is one of the most painful parts of my ministry. I find myself foolishly saying often, "God if I did not obey you, I would have been better off". I remember one day, the pressures of ministry were heavily weighing on me. For this reason, I desired some recreation. I told my mother I was going to go kayaking. Out of her fear for my mental health at the time, she requested that I go to a regular beach instead with a handful of friends. Although that is not what I wanted to do, I understood the importance of obedience to my elders, especially to my parents in the Lord (Ephesians 5:1). Two of my friends and I went to a beach that I have been to several times. When I go, I always park in the same spot. Five minutes after we went to the beach, it began to rain. As I ran back to my car, I realized it was not there. I thought it was stolen, but I learned it was towed. I did not know I was not allowed to park in that spot. I parked in the same place several times in the past year. I had to pay nearly $200 to get it back. Afterwards, I discovered that they scratched it while towing it. I instantly complained. I told myself that, "If I did not obey God or honor my mother, I would have been kayaking and this would not have happened". Joseph shares this testimony. He was thrown into a pit because he decided to obey his father. While doing something his father asked him to do in honor of God, that is when his brothers were able to take advantage of him (Genesis 37:14). He later was cast into prison for deciding to *not* sleep with a woman that was not his wife (Genesis 39).

Who Said You Are Doing Something Wrong?

If I were Joseph, I would question, "what am I doing wrong?" How is it possible for me to do the right thing and be under so much turmoil? Sometimes, the reason why you are going through your struggles is *because you are doing the right thing*. Job understood this. Job shared that, "Should we accept only good from God and not adversity?" (Job 2:10). Sections like this reveal the motivation as to why I wrote the book in the first place. As you complete your Kingdom assignment, adversity will come your way. Adversity doesn't always mean you are the problem. Persecution from the devil may mean you are a potential solution. The devil wants to stop you before you realize and become the answer that God created you to be for the world's problems.

Don't Stop Obeying

The season of persecution is an opportune time for the enemy to discourage you. During this season, the devil loves to tell me to stop what I am doing so I won't experience the pain of the ministry. The devil wears a disguise. The Bible says he dresses up as "an angel of light" (2 Corinthians 11:14). Whether it be him telling Eve to eat the fruit to become wise, or telling Jesus to turn stones into bread while He was hungry, the Devil always tries to appear beneficial. He wants you to think that he is helping you. For this reason, his words can be very enticing. Do not give in to them. There was a time when I told my Apostle, Errol Williams, that I wanted to stop running my youth ministry. His response was, "Too many lives are at stake". The devil is not stupid. He knows your assignment is a threat to him. That is the only reason why he is attacking you in the first place. I encourage you like the Apostle Paul encouraged Timothy to "endure afflictions" (2 Timothy 4:5). I also urge you to "Thou therefore endure hardness, as a good soldier of Jesus Christ" (2 Timothy 2:3). Being a soldier means you must understand spiritual warfare.

Joshua's Are Soldiers

Before Joshua became Moses' replacement, he was a captain in the army of Israel (Exodus 17:8). He led an army against the Amalekites. He was in the front of the battle. Similarly, walking as a young leader will cause you to be in the enemy's line of fire. You are vulnerable to persecution and demonic attacks. This is known as spiritual warfare. The first thing you have to understand is that spiritual warfare is *real*. When people refer to spiritual warfare, they are not being too deep. Instead, they are acknowledging a reality that is a threat to your destiny. Apostle Paul warned us that "We wrestle not against flesh and blood, but against principalities, against powers, against rulers of the darkness of this world, against spiritual wickedness in high places" (Ephesians 6:12). As we mentioned in Chapter 2, there are demonic spirits. These spirits, similarly to your spirit, not only have souls (a mind, will and emotions), but they also have assignments. In the same way God assigned you to the Earth to fulfill a purpose, these demons or demonic spirits are on the Earth to fulfill an assignment. Their assignment is to work against you.

While Joshua led that army against the Amelekites, he was not fighting alone. He had people fighting around him and people fighting above him. This is why Chapter 6 spoke about who you surround yourself with relationally. Your healthy spiritual friends represent those around you. Through mutual prayer and support, you all fight for one another. As I navigated many trials and tribulations, I had amazing friends who stuck beside me, prayed for me, and simply surrounded me with love. I thank God for these friends who helped me navigate calamity during my seasons of difficulty. Similarly, Joshua's spiritual father Moses was holding up a rod above him as he fought. I believe one of the reasons why I have been able to survive persecution is my *spiritual covering*: the individuals who have more spiritual experience than me and prioritize praying for me. This does not only refer to my pastors. This starts with my mother. I wrote this book during a time where I was charged with other spiritual responsibilities in addition to school. This season was a heavy season for me. Before I started this season, or even knew that this season was coming, my mother decided to spend a week fasting on my behalf. In obedience to God, she decided to cover me before she even knew what I needed covering for. This also includes my entire church, *New Alpha Worship Center*. I know for certain that there are intercessors who pray for me on a weekly, and even *daily* basis. They see the attacks before they come, and prophetically warn me to prepare for them so I will not be thrown off by them. This is why it is so important to not jump into ministry, especially at a leadership level, without being equipped. Because God wanted me to operate in my calling, He provided me with everything needed to sustain me in that calling. I know you want to go out and do what God has called you to do, but are you spiritually covered? Through leadership, God will tell you when it is your time to step out. I do not even take speaking engagements without asking my Apostle if it is okay for me to go out, because I know that he has the foresight from God to see if I am equipped for that assignment.

God Allows Warfare

Contrary to popular belief, God allows demons to work against you. An example of this is seen when Lazarus died in John 11. Jesus could have healed him before he died, but Jesus waited until after death to intervene. This lets us know that Jesus allowed Lazarus to experience death intentionally. In response to his condition, Jesus shared that, "This sickness is not unto death, but for the glory of God, that the Son of God might be glorified thereby" (John 11:4). Remember, the glory comes at a cost. Death is the cost of glory. God will allow demonic spirits to work against you, so some things can die within you. Until those things die in you, the glory will never be revealed through you. Paul instructed the church concerning a disobedient member to "Deliver such an one unto Satan for the destruction of the flesh, that the spirit may be saved in the day of the Lord Jesus" (1 Corinthians 5:5). The reality is, many people do not attempt to find God until they find problems in their personal lives. Your persecution might be God's way of getting you back into His presence. It should not be this way. However, we serve a God who wants you by any means necessary. If He created a storm and used a hungry, humongous fish to get Jonah's attention, what makes you think He will not allow persecution to solicit your repentance. Further evidence of this is seen in Hosea 2 when God wanted the children of Israel to repent. The Lord proclaimed, "Therefore, this is what I will do: I will block her way with thorns; I will enclose her with a wall, so that she cannot find her paths. She will pursue her lovers but not catch them; she will look for them but not find them. Then she will think, "I will go back to my former husband, for then it was better for me than now" (Hosea 2:6-7). In simpler terms, God used persecution to get Israel to return to Him. God knew that if Israel lost what they valued, they would return to God in their brokenness. God would rather you be broken and disgusted with Him than to have the things of this world and forget about Him. Jesus asked the question, "For what shall it profit a man, if he shall gain the whole world, and lose his own soul?" (Mark 8:36).

Devastation Or Attachment?

Persecution seasons are also known as seasons of devastation. This is for two reasons. First, they are seasons of total loss. Second, they are seasons that are depressive. After experiencing great loss during a persecution season, the Lord revealed to me that losing those things only hurt because *I had an unhealthy connection to them* in the first place. To illustrate, imagine if a shooter was targeting you. To protect you, I decided to kill that shooter. Would you be upset at me? Absolutely not! You would thank me for removing something that was threatening you. The reality is, we do not thank God for seasons of persecution because we do not realize that He is removing things that are threatening us. Paul commands us to thank God for everything because it is a part of God's divine plan for our lives (1 Thessalonians 5:18). If Joseph was not persecuted, he would not have been strategically shifted into the right places that catapulted his purpose. Your persecution is essential to your shift! You cannot stay stuck on this level. You cannot sit comfortable in a place you have outgrown. The pain moves you. There is purpose in your pain, do not let pain paralyze your purpose. Allow it to push you into what God has for you. As you go through it, you are becoming the person God desires you to be. Also, you end up going to the places He ordained for you to go.

Study War No More

There is a mystery in the scripture that many do not understand. A popular song named "Down By The Riverside," is the reason why this mystery is most familiar. In one section of that hymn, the singers boldly proclaim that they "ain't gon study war no more". This is actually taken from a prophecy about the future of Israel written in Isaiah. The prophet shared that, "He shall judge among the nations, and shall rebuke many people: and they shall beat their swords into plowshares, and their spears into pruning hooks: nation shall not lift up sword against nation, neither shall they learn war anymore" (Isaiah 2:4). This can be confusing. How can God say we will study war no more, when Ephesians 6 says we are wrestling against demonic entities. As mentioned in Chapter 7, we are not fighting the Devil. Jesus already defeated Him. We are fighting for our faith in the fact that Jesus defeated him. Paul elaborated on this by sharing that "For although we live in the flesh, we do not wage war according to the flesh, since the weapons of our warfare are not of the flesh but are powerful through God for the demolition of strongholds. We demolish arguments and every proud thing that is raised up against the knowledge of God, and we take **every thought captive** to obey Christ" (2 Corinthians 10:3-4). Not only is the battle spiritual, but it is more internal than external. It did not say that we take demons captive, but we take our own thoughts captive. It is not about fussing for hours in prayer with demons, but being intentional about keeping the faith that those demons are already under us (Luke 10:19). As a result of this, we do not have to study war. We do not have to learn how to fight demons. We have to fight to believe that we already have authority over them because of the victory of Jesus Christ. Evidence of this is seen in Moses. He did not have to prepare an army to fight against Pharoah. Instead, all he needed to do was keep believing in God. The *faith of Moses* caused the red sea to close in on his enemies (Exodus 14). Most battles in scripture were not about defeating the enemy but **believing God to defeat the enemy**. God told King Jehosaphat concerning one war that, "Ye shall not need to fight in this battle: set yourselves, stand ye still, and see the salvation of the Lord with you, O Judah and Jerusalem: fear not, nor be dismayed; tomorrow go out against them: for the Lord will be with you" (2 Chronicles 20:17). Change your mindset concerning warfare. You are not fighting a battle. You already won. Fight to believe that.

Study The Victory

Overcoming the season of persecution is all about faith. As mentioned in the previous chapter, faith is based on what you hear. Moses shared, "The Lord shall fight for you, and ye shall hold your peace" (Exodus 14:14). Many people think that this verse means, let the Lord fight the battle and leave it alone. Although that perspective is true, it is not the proper interpretation of this verse. In the proper context, this verse means that while the Lord is fighting for you, monitor what you say. Your words may be the reason why you do not make it out of persecution. The Bible says, "Death and life are in the power of the tongue: and they that love it shall eat the fruit thereof" (Proverbs 18:21). If you read the entire story of the children of Israel, especially the generation of Moses, you will find that as they went through trials, they continually wished death upon themselves. An example is found when they complained, "Because there were no graves in Egypt, hast thou taken us away to die in the wilderness? Wherefore hast thou dealt thus with us, to carry us forth out of Egypt?" (Exodus 14:11). Because they kept saying that they would die over and over, that is eventually what happened to the Moses generation. They got the fruit of their words. They all died before seeing the Promise Land. As a member of the Joshua generation, you are a new generation. This means you have a new mindset. You are not repeating the mistakes of the old generation but using them as opportunities to improve. Speak life! Meditate on the book of Psalms and recite some of them. During my seasons of persecution, I repeat this verse over and over: "I am certain that I will see the Lord's goodness in the land of the living" (Psalm 27:13 CSB). Declaring scriptures like these will be game changers in navigating the persecution season. They will make sure you do not quit. The King James Version of this verse says, "I had fainted, unless I had believed to see the goodness of the Lord in the land of the living" (Psalm 27:13). Another passage of scripture that speaks to me during my time of persecution is Psalm 73.

Don't Quit Before You Win

Your victory is guaranteed. The only thing that can get in the way of you is you. Your assignment does not stop because of tribulation.

Your assignment only stops if you quit because of the tribulation. As mentioned in the last chapter, what God says WILL come to pass. All His promises are yes and amen (2 Corinthians 1:20). It is not a matter of God doing it, but it is a matter of you agreeing with Him! Do you agree? The Devil persecutes you to stop your agreement. He knows that if there is not faith, or agreement with God, what God wants to do is limited by man's disbelief (Matthew 13:58). What are you going to do? I encourage you with the words of Apostle Paul: "Let us not be weary in well doing: for in due season we shall reap, if we faint not" (Galatians 6:9).

9

WHY ARE YOU RUSHING?

Once a believer is delivered from persecution, they experience a season of emancipation. This is when a believer experiences freedom from an oppressive season. The persecution finally comes to an end. Before you get excited, please be warned that the end of a season of persecution does not always indicate the beginning of a season of prosperity. A season of persecution can be followed by two types of seasons:

1. Another season of persecution: This was the case of Joseph. He left a pit for a slave house. After that, he left a slave house for a prison. He had more persecution to go through.

2. A season of postponement: A season where you are held back from your blessing by God because He wants to use it to develop character in you. This was the case of the children of Israel after leaving Egypt.

Not So Fast

The Children of Israel had already experienced many obstacles since Abraham received the assurance of the Promised Land. After hundreds of years of slavery and a tiresome fight for deliverance, you would think that God would finally allow them to rest in the Promised Land; however, that was not the case. Instead, scripture records God making an executive decision concerning them receiving the Promise Land. "When Pharaoh let the people go, God did not lead them along the road to the land of the Philistines, even though it was nearby; for God said, 'The people will change their minds and return to Egypt if they face war'" (Exodus 13:17 CSB). In simpler words, God could have taken an easier route to lead the children of Israel to the Promised Land. On the contrary, God did not do so because **they were not ready** to encounter the potential dangers that would meet them on that road. God decided to put them through a **wilderness** to prepare them for their promise. Do not be misled. Your exit from a tribulation is not an entrance to your prosperous, promised position. You may have to go through a season of postponement, so God can prepare you to be able to face your promise.

Season #4:Postponement

As a young leader, the moment you are anointed is not the moment you are put into the position. This is the case of David. He was anointed in 1 Samuel 16, but he did not become a king until 2 Samuel 5. Two important things to note. He did not become king until 20 chapters later; additionally, when he became king at that time, he only ruled over **one city** in the kingdom. This city was Judah. It was the city he originated from. He had to wait seven more years before he became king over all of Israel (2 Samuel 5:4). Imagine being in David's shoes. He had to wait for an extended period. Every time it looked like he would finally receive the promise God gave him, something else occurred that said, "Not yet". The wilderness is God's way of saying "not yet". The wilderness is assigned to prepare you for the promise.

Someone Is Already There

A major reason why the children of Israel could not inherit the Promised Land was because it was already occupied by another group of people: the Canaanites. The Israelites could not receive the land until it was time for these people to leave. I believe this is symbolic for Joshua type leaders. One error a young leader makes is trying to replace the person God set over them. Similar to someone already occupying the Promised Land, the position God promised you may be occupied by someone else right now. You are not meant to replace them while they are still in operation but follow after them. God will allow you to do so at an assigned time. Although David was told that he was going to be the king after Saul, he was not immediately able to take Saul's seat. There were valuable lessons he still needed to learn from Saul. As ready as he thought he was, he was not. The same goes for you. As ready as you think you are, God is not calling you to replace your leader right now. He is calling you to learn from your leader. Joshua did not even begin to take over Israel until Moses died. He was anointed while Moses was still alive, but he had to wait until Moses' assignment expired before he took over. If your goal is to replace your leader on the pulpit or make the decisions that he or she is making, that is not a godly goal. Maturing in your gift is not about running towards someone's position. It is about running towards God. As you pursue God, He will place you where you need to be without any help from you. There is no need to force your way there.

You Still Have An Assignment

At this moment, I want to make it clear that you are not assignment-less just because you are not doing your leader's assignment. Under your leader's assignment, you have an assignment that should further the goal of the assignment God gave your leader. I am a young leader at New Alpha Worship Center. My Apostle's assignment is to mature ministry gifts. While I am not maturing ministry gifts on the level and scale he is, I am evangelizing so he can have more ministry gifts to mature. Additionally, my pastor does not have the time or capacity to do everything, so anywhere I can assist him that he requests, I attempt to carry a piece of the heavy load. Doing so allows me to get **practice**. The wilderness was a place of practice. Before they conquered the Canaanites in the Promised Land, they practiced fighting other foreign groups in the wilderness. An example is the Amalekites that Joshua fought in Exodus 14. He fought some enemies under Moses' supervision before he fought some on his own after Moses' death. The same is the case for David. He fought Goliath and others under Saul's supervision before fighting the rest on his own after Saul's death. Practicing under your leader is critical. They can see what you are doing wrong and correct you. This ensures you do ministry properly. Before I preached or performed miracles, under the leading of Almighty God, at anyone else's church, I learned the proper protocol and requirements at my own church. This was facilitated

under the leadership and supervision of my apostle through teaching
and guided application.

A Joshua type of leader needs a leader that lets them practice, not a
leader who hogs all the glory. Sadly, not all leaders are like my pastor. I
want to take this moment to honor my leader, Apostle Errol Williams,
for his selfless approach towards ministry. He is not concerned about
building a personal name for his own glory, but "Equipping all Christ
followers to take the gospel around the world". That is the vision of
our church. For various reasons such as selfishness or innocent igno-
rance, some leaders think they must do **everything** in church. These
types of leaders do not encourage everyone under their leadership that
they have a purpose, nor do they give them opportunities to walk
in that purpose. Instead, they merely expect everyone to just serve
them as they walk in their own purpose. You walking in your own
purpose can be a threat to them. This was the case of Saul, who grew
jealous of David's success (1 Samuel 18:7-14). The most delusional
thing a young leader can do is assume that everyone will embrace you
as you walk in your assignment. The people you grow up in church
with will attempt to box you in because of familiarity. Jesus Christ
experienced this himself. In His hometown, they rejected His word
because they focused on His carnality instead of His anointing (Mark
6:4). People in your church may not see you as an anointed leader.
Instead, they may see a simple child. Don't grow discouraged. Paul
encouraged Timothy by commanding, "Don't let anyone despise your
youth, but set an example for the believers in speech, in conduct, in
love, in faith, and in purity" (1 Timothy 4:12). Another thing I am
still learning how to do is not take it personal. Too many times have I
let my emotions get in the way of my assignment. Hurt is not an excuse
to stop doing the will of God. The same people that hate you, you have
to love. The same people that curse you, you have to bless. The same

people that ignore you, you have to embrace. If you are not mature enough to do this, pray and ask God to help you. It is a requirement for your assignment. Read 2 Corinthians 4 to see how Paul managed this type of difficulty.

The Unknown Youth

One sad thing occurring in our churches is unfamiliarity. Because phenomenons are occurring that people are not used to, they instantly dismiss these new occurrences as demonic or out of order. Jesus was the first example of this. Religious people accused Him of being demonic and out of alignment with God because His methods and origin was foreign to them (Matthew 12:24). New has two definitions. The first is "something that was never done before". The second is "something that is different from what people are used to". It was not that Jesus was doing methods that were never done before. Instead, His methods were not currently in practice because religious systems drifted away from Christ's methodology. Jesus provides evidence to this by sharing that the religious people had distant hearts (Matthew 15:8).

The reality is, the Pharisees had a false ideology that the Messiah could only appear one type of way. The same stigmas are present in the church today. Saul told David that because he was just a youth", he could not fight Goliath (1 Samuel 17:33). David could not get the practice necessary for his assignment because Saul did not know he was more than just a youth. He did not know that David was anointed and experienced. Some young people in our churches today are not allowed to practice because the elders do not know them. Saul thought David was just a musician when he was introduced to him as a "man of war" (1 Samuel 16:18). Saul did not pay attention closely enough.

He was not invested or discerning enough to realize who David was; consequently, this resulted in him being unaware of David's potential. Some young people are deemed as just youths in church today as well. The elders over them are not invested or discerning enough to know that they are anointed and have experiences that qualify them to be used by God.

In order for the youth to be of God, they must dress a certain way, act a certain way, and sound a certain way. If they do not, then they are not in alignment with God and are not able to function in the church until they do. This is a false ideology. It is like Saul trying to fit David into his armor. If Saul prevented David from fighting Goliath because he was not wearing his armor, they would have lost a battle God ordained for them to win. My prayer for churches today is that they do not underestimate the power of a slingshot. We as young leaders may not be what they are used to, but we have oil on our lives too (Joel 2:28-29). I also pray churches understand that just because we do new things does not mean we reject old systems. David used his own slingshot to kill Goliath, but eventually he picked up Saul's sword to cut off Goliath's head. As young leaders, we cannot assume the elder generations have nothing for us. David picking up Saul's sword is symbolic of what God wants to do with His church. God wants an integration of generational practices. The elders must be willing to embrace the slingshot (the new practices of the youth) and the youth must be willing to pick up the sword (the foundational practices of the elders). The utilization of both will bring us into victory. Like Saul and David, we should not be in competition with one another. We should be like Moses and Joshua. We should be in collaboration with each other.

Know Your Place

In reference to your leaders, it is not your job to tell them how to execute their position as you are learning about it. Being young and anointed requires humility. You can think you know it all. I have to learn this every day. Sometimes, I foolishly think my methods are better than the execution of some of my church leaders. However, I must understand that God is a God of order. I am not saying that He will never give someone under a leader a message for the leader. There have been times where God has used me as a word of confirmation for my leadership. On the contrary, in terms of words of correction or new information, God can speak to them directly or through their voices of accountability. If my leader is in error, my job is to pray for him and pray for understanding because I do not know it all. God may be using them in a way that is beyond my rank. If anything needs to be corrected, the order of God will speak to them directly. He can also speak to their covering and accountability partners to give them that word. I do not have to worry about that. My job is to focus on my assignment and trust God. God even uses the mistakes of leadership for His honor and glory. The season of postponement is also a season of character development.

Fruits, Gifts, Titles

Recall that every door God opens for you is Him giving Himself a greater opportunity to be revealed through you. Because the devil understands this, open doors come with adversaries (1 Corinthians 16:19). Adversaries are not only the devil. They can also be difficult spiritual leaders or any other circumstance that resembles a wilderness that God put in your way. When it comes to determining if you are ready for the Promised Land, God is not concerned about how much the adversity is hurting you. Instead, He is concerned about how you respond to the adversity. Your response to adversity determines your trajectory.

True Spiritual Maturity

One of the reasons why some young Joshuas foolishly aim to replace their leaders is because they think a title is the goal of spiritual maturity. Spiritual maturity is not about increasing positionally but increasing characteristically. Character development is the true sign of spiritual maturation. A dose of the Spirit is all you need to operate in a gift, but maturity in the Spirit is required to demonstrate the character of God. The moment Saul was anointed and went in the company of prophets, he began to prophesy; however, he was not mature enough in the spirit to demonstrate the character of God (1 Samuel 10:10). You can fake a gift by copying others. You cannot fake character. This is why Jesus said you will know a tree by its fruits (Matthew 7:16). If you are looking at giftings to determine if someone is mature in the Spirit, you will easily be misled by wolves in sheep's clothing. However, the Bible tells us in Galatians 5 that true fruit or evidence of the Spirit is in godly character traits. They are love, joy, gentleness, kindness, meekness, patience, faith, goodness, and self-control (Galatians 5:22-23). One aspect of God quoted many times in scripture is, "I desire mercy and not sacrifice" (Hosea 6:6). He is not looking for leaders who go through the motions in a church through a familiar routine. God is looking for those who are dedicated to picking up their cross to reflect Christ under any circumstance. Are you okay with being uncomfortable for God? Review this passage of scripture:

Deuteronomy 8

2 Remember that the Lord your God led you on the entire journey these forty years in the wilderness, so that **he might humble you** *and test you to know what was in your heart, whether or not you would keep his commands. 3 He humbled you by letting you go hungry; then he gave you manna to eat, which you and your ancestors had not known, so that* **you might learn that man does not live on bread alone but on every word that comes from the mouth of the Lord.** *4 Your clothing did not wear out, and your feet did not swell these forty years. 5 Keep in mind that the Lord your God has been disciplining you just as a man disciplines his son "* (Deuteronomy 8:2-5 CSB).

The wilderness is **assigned uncomfortability from God** that requires you to depend on God. As a result of that dependence, you are subsequently processed to root out ungodly characteristics. In the wilderness, Israel had to let go of pride, disbelief, comparison, and low self-esteem, among other negative characteristics. If God did not root it out of them before He took them into the Promised Land, those same characteristics would have made them lose the Promised Land. So many different passages of scripture explain that pride is a sure way to lose what God has given you (Matthew 23:12). God puts you through a wilderness to root out distasteful characteristics before you receive your blessing, so you will not fumble your blessing after you receive it. It is like carbon experiencing heat and pressure. Overtime, it becomes a diamond. Compared to the length of a persecution season which is determined by God, the length of a wilderness season can be ***prolonged by you***. This is why it is known as a season of postponement. It begins with God postponing your promise to teach you a lesson. Eventually, you can become the postponer. You can hold your own self up by constantly failing the tests of christian character.

You are not allowed to skip developing the character of God. You will just go in circles until you do. Evidence that the Children of Israel postponed the wilderness is found when Moses shared, "It is an eleven-day journey from Horeb to Kadesh-barnea by way of Mount Seir" (Deuteronomy 1:2). An 11-day journey took them 40 years to get through (Numbers 14:34). It was not because God ordained for them to be there that long. Instead, it is a by-product of them failing the character tests. They were supposed to be humble and dependent on God, but they were prideful and led by themselves. As a result, they postponed their own promise.

God will not give you prosperity until you are ready. Stop looking for a mic and a stage and start looking for a chance to display the fruits of the Spirit. Because the children of Israel in Moses' generation never mastered the lesson of the wilderness, they died before the promise. Without character, you will not be able to see the promise. Even after you receive it, a lack of godly character can cause you to lose it. The Bible says that your gift will make room for you (Proverbs 18:16). On the contrary, bad character will kick you out and keep you out. As a young leader, remember that the goal is not to mature to a platform but to mature in the Spirit. We are not trying to be seen by more people, but we are trying to make sure more of Christ is seen in us. Christ is so much more than gifts, but a personality that the world needs to see more of. As you do ministry, the goal is to reflect that.

10

HOW DARE YOU SETLE?

Seasons of persecution and postponement are frustrating. If I had a choice, I would rather avoid them. Sadly, it is not that simple. Anything that I am unwilling to carry is something I ultimately abort. If I am not willing to carry the persecution and postponement that comes with my calling, I am rejecting the calling itself. If I hold on, I will receive what He promised me. It is like a baby being born. Jesus shared that, "A woman when she is in travail hath sorrow, because her hour is come: but as soon as she is delivered of the child, she remembereth no more the anguish, for joy that a man is born into the world" (John 16:21). Unlocking the anointing in your life is a birth. You are pregnant with purpose! You have to **PUSH** to bring it forward. Once a baby is born, the mother does not even remember the pain she went through in the delivery process. Similarly, once you unlock the anointing God has given you, the presence of new oil will cause you to forget the pain of the crushing. You only reap this benefit if you do not give up. The problem is, most Christians rather settle instead of travail. As God elevates you, the last chapter of this book is designed to make sure you do not get comfortable at a pit stop. Consider a connecting flight; If you get comfortable at the layover, you may miss the next flight to the assigned destination. Joshua type leaders are unlike the former generation. We do not want to stay in Egypt or die in the wilderness. We want to cross over the Jordan River and transition into the promise God gave us!

We Can Not Settle Here

Before Joshua became Israel's new leader, there was a group among the children of Israel who lost interest in crossing the Jordan. Because the land before the Jordan was beneficial for their cattle, they requested to settle there instead of the Promised Land (Numbers 32:4-5). Before we judge them, we have to admit that we can act just like them. The minute life gets good, especially after persecution and postponement, the sight of anything beneficial is enticing. Why do I need to pursue more when this is enough to satisfy me? One must pursue more because our God is a God of more. The Bible emphasizes that children of God should go "from glory to glory" (2 Corinthians 3:18). We should constantly advance into greater because the promise is greater than where we currently are.

Season #5: Prosperity

Recall the story of Joseph. Similarly to the children of Israel, he experienced the five spiritual seasons. First, he received a promise that his family would bow down to him. Second, he was privileged by his father with a coat of many colors. Third, he was persecuted in a pit, on a plantation, and in a prison. Fourth, he experienced postponement as he awaited deliverance from the prison. The fifth and final season is entitled prosperity.

Prosperity is the state of receiving the promise after seasons of persecution and postponement. This is what the persecution and postponement was preparing you for. Many preachers, when they elaborate on the story of Joseph, mostly focus on him going from "the pit to the palace". The highlight tends to be on his promotion. As young leaders, there are a few lessons about prosperity that we can learn from the promotion of Joseph.

1. Our prosperity is dependent on our service in difficult seasons.

Many stop serving when their current state of life is unbeneficial. Joseph's escape from prison was because he continued to serve the Lord in his pain. Let me be clear. I am not telling you to continue praying and ministering to people while you are broken. A wise person told me that if you minister to people while you are broken, you will bleed on people who did not cut you. This is why the previous chapter emphasized the importance of having the proper character, so when you bear fruit or minister to others, it will not leave a bitter taste in their mouth. I am telling you to not use the pain as an excuse to stop seeking God and growing in your calling. Despite being in a prison, Joseph continued to seek after God and encourage himself in the Lord, so he can progress in his calling and develop his gifts. This is what enabled him to interpret the dreams of the baker and cupbearer in prison. If he had not interpreted those dreams, God would have been unable to use the cupbearer as a way to get him out of prison (Genesis 40-41). The reality is, you do not need to be in a prosperous position to serve God, seek God, and perform His will. You can do His will in whatever condition you are in, as long as you are being restored by His spirit through intentionally seeking Him. Because Joseph was sold out to God, he did not use his personal discomfort as an excuse to quit searching for God. This enabled him to be equipped to be used by God. Prosperity is only for those who do not make excuses, because obedience is what propels you into prosperity.

2. Our prosperity is dependent on our ability to give God the glory.

When Joseph was invited to interpret Pharaoh's dream, he told Pharaoh, "I am not able to, it is God who will give Pharaoh a favorable answer" (Genesis 41:16 CSB). This type of humility is what made Joseph an ideal candidate for prosperity. We have been emphasizing that God opens doors for Himself to be revealed. Joseph is the epitome of the type of heart God is looking for. This type of heart is one that God can trust. God will prosper anybody who He can trust. As a young leader, ask yourself this question: Can God trust me?

While the palace is an amazing part of Joseph's story, I would like to argue that him becoming Pharaoh's second in charge was not his full prosperity. It was just a stepping stone in him becoming prosperous. Many preachers end their sermon on that point, but God did not end His journey with Joseph at that point. **Prosperity from God is not just receiving benefits but receiving the promise**. While Joseph was promoted to the palace in Genesis 41, he entered into true prosperity in the next chapter. When his brothers needed him to eat in the middle of a famine, Joseph entered into his promise. This was the fulfillment of the dreams he had in Genesis 37 where his entire family bowed to him. The same brother they threw in the pit is the reason why they are able to survive in a famine. **True prosperity is purpose centered**. Being blessed is not enough. There are so many who are blessed yet they are not prosperous. You should not just settle for a blessing. You should be the blessing to others with your blessings. That is the evidence of a prosperous believer.

Show A Christ-Like Nature In Your Favor

This is why we go through a season of postponement. Until we develop a Christlike character, we are not equipped to properly respond in the season of prosperity. Being like Christ means to love those who do not love in return. Christ loves the same people who put Him on the cross. Joseph loved the brothers who threw him in the pit, to the point where he let them eat at his table. Everyone loves quoting that God "Prepares a table before me in the presence of my enemies" (Psalm 23:5 CSB). However, the table is intentional. A table means that there are seats. God gives you a table in the presence of your enemies so you give them a seat at the table and feed them like Joseph. True biblical prosperity is more than merely receiving benefits. It is about receiving the promise of God so you can be a blessing to others, including your enemies. Life may be good right now, but have you been a blessing to anybody else?

Joshuas Divide The Blessing

Over the course of this book, we learned about the different functions of Joshua. He served as Moses' armor bearer, a military leader, and eventually their guide into the Promised Land. Joshua was responsible for pointing them to the blessing. Joshua also had to be the property manager. He divided the blessing that was received. The same Joseph gave land to his brothers in Egypt, Joshua divided the land each tribe should receive (Joshua 13:9). Financial management is attached to the Joshua anointing.

In order for Joseph and Joshua to reach their prosperity, God needed to trust them economically. Because their anointing was attached to provision and property, God had to ensure they would properly manage it. If they could not manage it, they would have been unable to do the will of God with what He gave them. How could God trust Joseph to feed the world, if he could not manage the little he had? How could God trust Joshua to divide the Promised Land, if he could not properly manage a few dollars? Similarly, in order for me to write this book, I had to show God that I was trustworthy enough to manage the funds that He would give me to publish it. As the leader of a youth ministry, God trusted me to manage thousands of dollars that have been sown into our ministry so far. God examines the way I handle my personal finances to determine if I can handle ministry prosperity. In regards to Joseph, during seasons of persecution and postponement, God was examining his management ability. God promoted him to the manager of Potiphar's house and the prison so he can get financial management practice. God was testing if he was a faithful steward. Joseph passed the test. Are you passing the test?

Passing The Financial Test

The first way to pass the financial test is to tithe. In Malachi 3, God expressed his disdain that people do not bring their tithes into the house of God (Malchi 3:10). As a believer, no matter your age, you should give 10% of the money you make to your local church. This reveals that you obey the word of God with your money.

The second way to pass the financial test is to exhibit wisdom. This is an area that I still struggle in, and I am requesting your prayer on my behalf in regards to this. There are two categories of wisdom according to scripture (James 3, 1 Corinthians 3). One wisdom is worldly and motivated by the flesh. The other is led by the Spirit through obeying the voice of God. You should not splurge on everything you want, but you should invite God into every financial decision you make. This will mean that sometimes you cannot purchase what you prefer. Doing so will demonstrate to God that you are someone He can trust. Based on your current spending habits, can God give you one million dollars to do ministry? As for me, I am not ready. Sadly, I may spend most of that money on food. Again, keep me in your prayers.

The third way to pass the financial test is generosity. Joseph was blessed to bless his brothers and all of Egypt. The reality is, many people are stingy. Pastor Michael Todd shares that, "God gives money to you to send it through you".[1] YouthForChrist305+, the youth ministry that I lead, has been a financial blessing to many other ministries near and far to us. We are not a stingy ministry, because we understand that we are blessed to be a blessing. There are stipulations to being generous. First, only give because God told you to. Do not just give away all your money for generosity's sake. That is poor financial management. Second, generosity must be from a pure heart. When our youth ministry gives, we do not do it for attention or to impress who we give it to. We do it because we want to please God. This leads into the last point. Lastly, generosity must be secret. According to the Bible, your generosity is not a social media moment (Matthew 6:3). We do not give so we can go viral. We give to obey God. Following these steps will show God that you are trustworthy to manage financial resources. He will supply you with the money and other capital need-

---

1. From Pastor Michael Todd Paper Chasers Series on Youtube at Transformation Church

ed to execute the visions He gave you. Members of my local church, New Alpha Worship Center, alongside other members in the body of Christ, sewed over $1000 into the publication of this book **without me asking them**. I nearly let not having enough money stop me from writing it. I considered getting a job to finance it, but God wanted to do it. He wanted to be the only One who received credit for the publication. At this moment, I give God all the glory for financing this book. I also give Him the glory for every word His Spirit inspired to edify you.

True Biblical Prosperity

God does not just care about our spiritual prosperity, but our prosperity in every area. According to the Bible, God wants us to holistically "prosper even as our soul prospers" (3 John 1:2). It is not only about being saved. Our spiritual prosperity should transcend to our soul and body. As you do the work of God and grow into the calling He has on your life, **do not sacrifice your mental health**. When I first founded my youth ministry, I did not have any balance. I experienced sleep deprivation, anxiety, and depression. I had to analyze where I was going wrong and make the proper adjustments. A mentally frustrated person is a person that God cannot use to His desired potential. Now, I make sure I get proper sleep at night. I also went to therapy to learn coping mechanisms so I can reduce anxious and depressive episodes. This ensured that I am in the best mental state for God to use me. Similarly, as you do the work of God, do not sacrifice your physical health. God cannot use a body that is limited by a hospital bed. To grasp a better understanding of this, I recommend reading *Struck by the Silent Killer* by Errol Williams.

There Is More Work To Do

We have come to the end of this book, but not the end of your journey. As you can see, there is a lot of work for both you and I to do. Never can we say that we have arrived. There is constant work for us to do internally and externally. Nevertheless, we shall press on because it is all for His glory. As the author of this book, I am still unlocking the Joshua anointing in my own life. Because of how many mistakes I make, I feel like giving up right where I am sometimes. That is the perfectionist nature in me. I feel like if I cannot do it perfectly, I cannot do it at all. **Perfection is NOT the standard to be used by God. Submission is the standard to be used by God**. As imperfect as I am, my submission to God allows Him to make a masterpiece out of broken pieces. For this reason, like the Apostle Paul, "I press toward the mark for the prize of the high calling of God in Christ Jesus" (Phillipians 3:14). Other versions refer to the high calling as the promise. That promise that was spoken over you before you were born, pursue it! As you go through all the difficult seasons, remember that they are critical to your development. Boast in the pain! Paul shared that, "We also boast in our afflictions, because we know that affliction produces endurance, endurance produces proven character, and proven character produces hope. This hope will not disappoint us" (Romans 5:3-5). You will not be disappointed when you see where God is taking you. As you unlock what God put on the inside of you, the world will be changed because of the great things God ordained and empowered you to accomplish! In conclusion, don't settle! Attending church is not enough! Being saved is not enough! How dare you settle? The Bible shares that, "Today is a day of distress, rebuke, and disgrace, for children have come to the point of birth, but there is no strength to deliver them" (2 Kings 19:3 CSB). In other words, it is a terrible thing to be pregnant with something from God and sit on it. It must come forth. I pray right now that every anointing on the inside of you will come forth according to the will of God. I pray that God will grant you the strength to successfully overcome every difficult season, so you will not give up before the birth. Lastly, I pray that you will remain humble and submitted to the spirit of God, so He can position you in the place where He desires to prosper you. Amen.

PROPHETIC CHARGE

RELEASE YOUR SOUND!

B efore you go out and walk in the calling that God has given you, the last concept that I want to leave you with is the importance of sound!

Sound is the "the ideas and impressions conveyed by words"; more specifically, sound is what comes out of your mouth.

First, Joshua generation leaders differ from the leaders of the Moses generation because of the **presence of sound**. If you look at the early life of Moses in Exodus 3-4, you will find that he denied the opportunity to speak on behalf of God because of his stuttering problem (Exodus 4:10). Instead, he asked God to use someone else (Exodus 4:13). As a result, Moses had an **ABSENT sound**. He was a whispering prophet. He did not have the boldness to open his own mouth. Joshua was different. He did not request for a mouth piece. He embraced being God's mouth piece. Second, those in the Joshua generation differ from those in the Moses generation because of the **agreement of their sound**. Because sound is a reflection of an idea, it is also the reflection of a mindset. The sound one releases will indicate what they are thinking. The people of the Moses' generation constantly murmured against what God was doing (Exodus 16:2). They had a **CONTRARY sound** to what God was doing. Further evidence of this is seen in Numbers 13 and 14 when ten out of twelve spies brought back negative reports concerning the promise land. By implying that the children of Israel were unqualified to receive the promise land, they released a sound that was contrary to what God was doing. On the other hand, the Joshua generation is not recorded murmuring in the way that the Moses generation did. While ten spies brought back bad reports, two spies from the Joshua generation named Joshua and Caleb brought back good reports. They saw the need to believe in what God said and follow suit with what He is doing. Their sound indicated unity with God. Lastly, the Joshua generation had a **submitted sound** before God. In contrast, the Moses generation did not care about what they said, and how their words offended God. They did not consider their words to be an offering unto the Lord: something that He heard from heaven and received or rejected. The Bible shares that God responded to the murmuring, Moses generation, "the Lord heard the sound of your words, and He was angry and took an oath, saying, 'Not one of these men, this evil generation, shall see the good land which I swore (solemnly promised) to give to your fathers" (Deuteronomy 1:34-35 AMP). A person whose sound is not dictated by the Spirit of God is a person who is ineligible to receive from God. If He can not trust your mouth to yield to Him, that means the glory He allows you to experience at every open door will not be given bak to Him. The Moses' generation had a **defiant sound.** On the contrary, one famous quote from Joshua includes "but as for me and my house, we will serve the Lord!" (Joshua 24:15). Joshua made it clear that his generation was a yielded generation before God. They do not say anything unless God tells them to speak. Like Ezekiel, they become dumb (unable to speak) unless God urges them to open their mouth (Ezekiel 3:26-27). When they do speak, they are only saying what thus saith the Lord! What generation are you a part of? Your sound is evidence of Whose you are. If your a child of God, you have a sound!

John 3:8

The wind blows where it pleases, and you hear its sound, but you don't know where it comes from or where it is going. So it is with everyone born of the Spirit.

Sound is caused by vibrations.
Vibrations are known for shaking things up.

We serve a God who is a shaker. Jesus made this clear when He shared that, "Don't assume that I came to bring peace on the earth. I did not come to bring peace, but a sword" (Matthew 10:34 CSB). This means that Jesus did not come softly to fit in to the wickedness of this world. Jesus came aggressively to disturb the sinful world system and bring it back to God's original order and intent. He does not accomplish this by being silent. Sound is required to shake things. In reference to this, the Bible shares that, "His [God's] voice shook the Earth" (Hebrews 12:26 CSB). The sound from the voice of God is compared to thunder (Psalm 29:3-5). Whenever the word of God is spoken, the sound that is released causes a shaking in the Earth. It brings life; "I assure you and most solemnly say to you, a time is coming and is [here] now, when the dead will hear the voice of the Son of God, and those who hear it will live" (John 5:25 AMP).

As God's mouthpieces, God is expecting us to release a sound similar to His sound. The sound is meant to shake our generation and our territory. If there is no sound, there is no change. The sound serves two purposes. First, it initiates the change. Second, it is evidence of the change. You are not allowed to move until you receive your sound. In the book of Acts, Jesus told the disciples to wait until their sound was released before they start ministry (Acts 1:4). They met daily for prayer (Acts 1:13-14). Prayer is a "preliminary sound". You cannot release a sound if your mouth is closed. The fact that they opened their mouths daily in prayer was evidence that they were preparing to release a greater sound. One day as they were praying, the Bible records "suddenly a sound like that of a violent rushing wind came from heaven, and it filled the whole house where they were staying" (Acts 2:2 CSB). This sound came from the Spirit of God. Because the Spirit has a sound, and they received the Spirit, they also received the sound of the Spirit and started to speak in new tongues (Acts 2:4). The release of this sound caused a shaking in their midst. First, it ignited change within their community. The disciples were elevated from being mere followers of Christ, to being the body of Christ. They became His church, who were His hands and feet on the Earth. Not only that, their sound was evidence that they different to those outside of their community. Those who were not in the room with them became curious about them because of their sound. This led them to go inquire what was that sound and where it was coming from. As a result, 3,000 souls were saved all because of the sound of a generation. A new generation emerged with a sound that shook their environment.

Similarly, when the Joshua generation was getting ready to cross over into their Promised land, God asked them to present a sound. God wanted the sound to agree with what He was doing, and submit to when and how He wanted it. They obeyed and their obedience produced results. The Bible shares that, "The troops shouted, and the rams' horns sounded. When they heard the blast of the ram's horn, the troops gave a great shout, and **the wall collapsed**. The troops advanced into the city, each man straight ahead, and they captured the city (Joshua 6:20).

I HEARD THE LORD SAY THAT **CLOSED MOUTHS WILL NOT GET FED IN THIS SEASON.** GOD IS LOOKING FOR A GENERATION THAT HAS A **SOUND TO RELEASE** IN THE EARTH. HE IS NOT LOOKING FOR AN ORDINARY SOUND EITHER. HE IS LOOKING FOR A SOUND FROM PEOPLE **BAPTIZED WITH THE HOLY GHOST**. HE IS LOOKING FOR THE SOUND OF THE **JOSHUA GENERATION.** WHERE IS THE PRESENT SOUND? WHERE IS THE AGREEING SOUND? WHERE IS THE SUBMITTED SOUND? FOR WHEN THAT SOUND IS RELEASED, SAITH THE LORD, **IT WILL SHAKE THE EARTH.** THAT SOUND IS **AN AMPLIFICATION OF ME,** SO THE SAME WAY MY VOICE SHAKES, I HAVE EMPOWERED THIS GENERATION WITH A **SOUND TO SHAKE THE WORLD!**

THE SOUND WILL BE THE WAY YOU TAKE IT BY FORCE! YOUR SOUND WILL GIVE YOU ACCESS TO THE SPOILS BY BREAKING DOWN WALLS OF DEMONIC HINDRANCE!
RELEASE THE SOUND
WATCH THE WALLS COME DOWN

IN JESUS NAME

September 6, 2023

www.ingramcontent.com/pod-product-compliance
Lightning Source LLC
Chambersburg PA
CBHW060331130626
46553CB00003B/976